ISBN 978-1-333-55438-5
PIBN 10519073

English
Français
Deutsche
Italiano
Español
Português

www.forgottenbooks.com

Mythology Photography **Fiction**
Fishing Christianity **Art** Cooking
Essays Buddhism Freemasonry
Medicine **Biology** Music **Ancient
Egypt** Evolution Carpentry Physics
Dance Geology **Mathematics** Fitness
Shakespeare **Folklore** Yoga Marketing
Confidence Immortality Biographies
Poetry **Psychology** Witchcraft
Electronics Chemistry History **Law**
Accounting **Philosophy** Anthropology
Alchemy Drama Quantum Mechanics
Atheism Sexual Health **Ancient History**
Entrepreneurship Languages Sport
Paleontology Needlework Islam
Metaphysics Investment Archaeology
Parenting Statistics Criminology
Motivational

LOST CERTIFICATES

OF

KNIGHT'S FEES

For the Counties of Nottingham and Derby,

FROM THE COPIES PRESERVED IN

THE RED BOOK OF THE EXCHEQUER

WITH

OBSERVATIONS RESPECTING THEIR DATE AND HISTORY.

REPRINTED FROM

"The Feudal History of the County of Derby,"

(*Chiefly during the 11th, 12th, and 13th Centuries,*)

BY

JOHN PYM YEATMAN, ESQ.,

(*Of Lincoln's Inn, Barrister-at-Law, formerly of Emmanuel College, Cambridge, and F.R.H.S., &c.*)

AUTHOR OF "THE EARLY GENEALOGICAL HISTORY OF THE HOUSE OF ARUNDEL;" "THE HISTORY OF THE COMMON LAW OF GREAT BRITAIN AND GAUL;" "AN INTRODUCTION TO THE STUDY OF EARLY ENGLISH HISTORY;" "THE MAYOR'S COURT ACT, 1857;" "AN INTRODUCTION TO THE HISTORY OF THE HOUSE OF GLANVILLE;" "A TREATISE ON THE LAW OF TRADES MARKS;" "THE ORIGIN OF THE NATIONS OF WESTERN EUROPE;" "THE RECORDS OF CHESTERFIELD;" "A TREATISE ON THE LAW OF ANCIENT DEMESNE;" "THE DOMESDAY BOOK FOR THE COUNTY OF DERBY;" "THE PIPE ROLLS FOR THE COUNTIES OF NOTTINGHAM AND DERBY;" "AN EXPOSURE OF THE MISMANAGEMENT OF THE PUBLIC RECORD OFFICE," ETC., ETC.

London:

BEMROSE & SONS, 23, OLD BAILEY; AND DERBY.

LONDON AND OXFORD: PARKER & Co.

CHESTERFIELD: WILFRED EDMUNDS, "DERBYSHIRE TIMES."

THE
LOST CERTIFICATES

OF

KNIGHT'S FEES

for the Counties of Nottingham and Derby,

FROM THE COPIES PRESERVED IN

THE RED BOOK OF THE EXCHEQUER,

WITH

OBSERVATIONS RESPECTING THEIR DATE AND HISTORY.

REPRINTED FROM

"The Feudal History of the County of Derby,"

(*Chiefly during the 11th, 12th, and 13th Centuries,*)

BY

JOHN PYM YEATMAN, ESQ.,

(*Of Lincoln's Inn, Barrister-at-Law, formerly of Emmanuel
College, Cambridge, and F.R.H.S., &c.*)

AUTHOR OF "THE EARLY GENEALOGICAL HISTORY OF THE HOUSE OF ARUNDEL;" "THE HISTORY OF THE COMMON LAW OF GREAT BRITAIN AND GAUL;" "AN INTRODUCTION TO THE STUDY OF EARLY ENGLISH HISTORY;" "THE MAYOR'S COURT ACT, 1857;" "AN INTRODUCTION TO THE HISTORY OF THE HOUSE OF GLANVILLE;" "A TREATISE ON THE LAW OF TRADES MARKS;" "THE ORIGIN OF THE NATIONS OF WESTERN EUROPE;" "THE RECORDS OF CHESTERFIELD;" "A TREATISE ON THE LAW OF ANCIENT DEMESNE;" "THE DOMESDAY BOOK FOR THE COUNTY OF DERBY;" "THE PIPE ROLLS FOR THE COUNTIES OF NOTTINGHAM AND DERBY;" "AN EXPOSURE OF THE MISMANAGEMENT OF THE PUBLIC RECORD OFFICE," ETC., ETC.

London:

BEMROSE & SONS, 23, OLD BAILEY; AND DERBY.

LONDON AND OXFORD: PARKER & Co.

CHESTERFIELD: WILFRED EDMUNDS, "DERBYSHIRE TIMES."

SECTION II.

COLLECTIONS FOR THE HISTORY OF DERBYSHIRE.

THE RED BOOK OF THE EXCHEQUER

FOR THE

COUNTIES OF NOTTINGHAM AND DERBY.

CHAPTER III.

THE Red Book of the Exchequer is a volume of rare value and authority, although it is admittedly only a copy of certain very ancient records which were kept in the Exchequer, most of which have long since disappeared. One only of the whole class of certificates of knights' fees has escaped destruction. Madox refers to it, and it can be found at the Record Office, classified as a "seal." In appearance, it in no way differs from an ordinary charter of the period.

Like Domesday, the Red Book is a purely fiscal document, and its chief value consists in the fact that it gives full particulars of certain records of which only the summaries are given in the Pipe Rolls. The greater part of the book is occupied with extracts from the Pipe Rolls, made no doubt for the convenience of the officers of the Exchequer; but these are of small practical value, since they are neither so full nor so accurate as the originals, and therefore, when they differ, must be summarily rejected ; but the portions of the book here given are of the highest value, because the originals are lost, and we have no other evidence of their contents. They do possess partly the character of original documents, in the same way that the " Record" in a law suit is an original document, although in fact it is only a copy of the pleadings. These copies were no doubt used by the officers of the Exchequer for the purposes of assessment. Herne, in his collections, has published the valuable portion of this book, and of the copy of it called the Black Book (why so called it is not known, possibly to distinguish between the books, one of which was probably kept in the Chancery, and the other in the Exchequer) ; and it is now proposed to publish the whole of it ; but inasmuch as the Pipe Roll Society has undertaken to give those portions from the original, this seems to be not only unnecessary, but unfortunate, since it is always a mistake to propagate erroneous accounts.

The author has already given the portion of the Red Book which is copied from the Pipe Rolls, and proposes now only to give that which supplements it—namely, the particulars of the fees of the greater barons, and, unfortunately, only a portion of them are here to be found, proof that this collection was made at a late date, when some of this class of documents were lost. It is very difficult to assign a precise date to any of these records, but this is clear, that the commonly received idea that they were returned for the scutage levied upon the marriage of the daughter of King Henry the Second is a false one, for some of them date long afterwards.

This is absolutely clear, from the certificate of Wm. Briwere, who, as it will be shown in the parochial history, had no connection with Derbyshire until about the fifth year of King Richard I., when he was Regent. Chesterfield was one of the manors of the ancient demesne ·of the Crown, and prior to that date was farmed by the hospital of lepers at that place, as appears from the Pipe Rolls of this date ; so, too, other returns show that some of the barons appearing were dead at that period. Again, it is abundantly clear that several scutages were assessed from the same record, and that a scutage was frequently used long after some of the knights apparently living were dead ; and it is only when we come to the age of King Henry III. that any note of this appears upon the face of the record itself. The scutage lists were corrected just as Domesday was made on the Itinerary of the justices ; and this, too, is apparent, that a fresh certificate would be only required when there was a change of tenure, and not upon the occasion of successive taxations, and this return would probably last for the life of the baron who made it, when his successor would make a new one, and the old one would be discarded.

The aid for marrying the king's daughter was levied in the 14th year of his reign (see page 109) ; and the order in which the knights are named is different from the order of this document, although, with the exception of the name of Warner de Insula appearing in the first, and that of William Briwere in his place in the second, they are identical. The brethren of the hospital are in this record charged for the ½ fee held subsequently by William Briwere.

It is quite clear, therefore, from this comparison that these certificates were not made for the scutage of the 14th Henry II.

Madox gives a note from a Pipe Roll two years earlier, showing that the certificates of the knights' fees were then kept in the county (probably only the duplicate copy), for a hutch is made to receive them. This shows that some were made prior to 14th Henry II., just as William Briwere's certificate shows that some were made subsequently ; and this also establishes the fact that they were made at different times. The strong probability is, that they were made when there was occasion for them, that is, when seizin was given to the new baron. The value of this fact is of wider import than Derby shire history, for this assumed date has been acted upon for centuries, and consequently numerous well-known pedigrees are wrongly dated.

The Close Rolls show that on every scutage a writ was addressed to the greater baron to enable him to make his own return, as well as to the sheriff, to return for the lesser holders, and for those great barons whose estates were in the king's hands ; but this does not necessarily imply that a fresh certificate was given upon each occasion, but only another payment.

The Pipe Rolls show only two other scutages in the reign of Henry II., one in the eighth year of the king, and that of those who did not go with the king's army into Galway, in the thirty-third year of the king, when Hasculf Musard was dead,

and it is generally assumed that there were no other scutages
in his reign, but it should rather be considered that those
assessments were of an extraordinary character, and that the
certificates of· knights' fees were made, not only for them, but
for all other exactions of the exchequer, for Danegeld, and
the annual farm of the county. In fact, that just as the
sheriff made returns for the purposes of scutage upon the
inquests taken before the Justices Itinerant from, and including,
the date of Domesday, so those barons who were privileged to
make their own returns, corrected the charters of their own
baronies at the same periods, if it was found necessary to do so.

In the second year of Henry II. (see page 100), we find
mention of a great variety of payments. Danegeld for both
counties, £38 5s.; Burgess aid, £15; Gift of the county,
80 m. ; Farm of the county, £123 14s. 1d., and rents of the
king's manors for the whole of the county, £180 14s.   This
does not include forfeited estates, for £103 18s. 6d. was received
for Wm. Peverel's lands, and £94 6s. 2d. for the rents of his
manors ; for many of these purposes the same assessment would
be requisite.

In 4 Henry II. (page 104), the sheriff accounted for £93 6s. 8d.
for the gift of the county, which was evidently a regular levy,
for the names of some who were excused payment are given.

In 5 Henry II., p. 104, the sheriff again accounted for £168
of the gift of the county.

In the sixth year, the Earl of Ferrars' estate was in the king's
hands, and in the following year there was evidently an assessment ; and in the eighth of the king both a scutage and
Danegeld were levied ; in fact, payments of some kind were
exacted nearly every year. It is rash, therefore, to assign a
particular date for a series of documents which were in constant
requisition for a variety of purposes ; and the safe conclusion
seems to be that they were made when they were wanted,
that is, upon a change of tenancy ; and the only certainty seems
to be that they were made under the old system of taxation
derived from and laid down in Domesday, before it was altered
by Archbishop Hubert Walter in 1198. It is highly probable,
though it cannot be put higher, that the Archbishop caused
this collection of documents to be recorded for the purposes of
the new assessment, and that they were recopied with the

muniments of a later date—when the present Red Book was composed.

We shall find, when we come to the Testa de Nevil, that the privilege of the greater barons in making their own assessments, or returns, was highly valued, and that it was the subject of fierce contention. No doubt it was also profitable, as well as honourable, to be independent of the sheriff, and consequently the privilege was religiously guarded and preserved.

The returns for the Counties of Nottingham and Derby are given together, since as the names of the manors held by the several knights are not given, it is impossible to separate them. We only possess the returns made by the Earl of Ferrars, Ralf Anselin, Robert de Chaus, Ralf fitz William, Hubert fitz Ralf, Roger de Buron, and Hasculf Musard, only seven for both counties out of a total of thirty-two barons and abbots of the time of Domesday, and only four of these barons were certainly descended in the male line from the Domesday holder.

The return, however, of the Earl Ferrars, is of the greatest value, more especially since he divides it into three distinct periods : those knights who were enfeoffed by the Domesday holder, the ancestor of his grandfather, those enfeoffed by his grandfather, and those of his father's feoffment. This return takes us back, as respects the greater part of the county, to Domesday itself, and as to the second portion, to a period commencing within two years, for Robert de Ferrars, son of the Domesday Baron, flourished from the year 1088 to the year 1139, four years after the death of Henry I. His son, Robert de Ferrars, flourished from 1139 to 1162, in which year William de Ferrars, who made the return, came into the possession of his barony. His return, therefore, could not have been made earlier than this latter year, though, probably, very soon after, for he had made no alteration amongst his knights. It will be observed that the vast majority of the earl's retainers were enfeoffed by the ancestor of Robert de Ferrars, that is, prior to 1088, and that, in most cases, the descent of the land is given to the date of his great grandson.

Now, considering that Henry de Ferrars held no less than 114 manors in Derby alone, and that many of his knights held lands under other barons, it will be seen that this return covers a most important portion of the county, in fact, the greatest part of it, and doubtless, nearly every one of these knights have left descendants collateral or direct, who now survive, and form the staple of the people of the county, though, in most instances, their descendants, having adopted local names, have lost all memory and trace of their names and descent.

Henry Ferrars, the chief landowner of the County of Derby at Domesday, was of a Norman family, who were of the most distinguished position, both in Normandy and England. He was the son of Vauqueline, or Walkelin (as the name is written in England), Lord of Ferrieres St. Hilaire, near Bernai, where, even in those days, he had great ironworks. His descendants bore the curious title of Premiers Barons Fossiers de Normandie. It is perhaps not singular that Henry, son of Vauqueline de Ferrars, should obtain the lordship of one of the chief mining districts in England. As an instance of the keenness of the family for mines, Robert de Ferrars, in the first Pipe Roll, pays £80 for the farm of Wirksworth, where the king had no less than three leadworks, and the large amount of rent paid shows their value. Vauqueline de Ferrars perished in one of those lawless feuds which marred the minority of Duke William. He and Hugh de Montforte sur Risle, the son of Toustain de Bastemburg, one of the most proud and violent of the Norman nobility, levied war upon each other, and both of them perished in the murderous affray. As this occurred about 1035 or 36, Henry de Ferrars could not have been a young man at the time of the conquest of England. He is perhaps best known as one of the Commissioners who compiled Domesday for the circuit in which his property lay; that is, that as one of the greatest personages of his circuit, the ancient kingdom of Mercia, he was employed as one of the king's Justices Itinerant. Modern writers are pleased to assert that Justices Itinerant and their circuits was an invention of several centuries later; but a series of documents show that they did exactly the same work as the Domesday Commissioners, in addition to the work of the Aula Regis; in fact, that this part of the work of the Domesday Commissioners was, and continued to be a part, and a very material part, of the regular duties of the Justices Itinerant, and that the circuits they travelled which were coterminous with the ancient kingdoms into which England was divided, practically agree with the divisions of the circuits of the present day.

We possess, in a document to be given presently (a fragment), a specimen of the mode in which scutages were assessed. This is called Kirby's Quest ; and the only difference between the method pursued in it and in Domesday is that, in the later documents, or assize records, only the lesser baronies are detailed. The great barons, probably on account of their high rank, made their own returns to the king by their own charters, under their own hands and seals, which are given here as certificates of knights' fees. It will be seen that the scutage lists of the Pipe Rolls give no particulars of the great fiefs here given, so that they are, in fact, a supplement to those records. We invariably learn this from the Pipe Rolls, and no more, that the Earl of Derby answered for 68½ fees. Here, for the first time, we obtain particulars of his holding ; so the fees of Hubert fitz Ralf of Domesday, of Ralf Hanselin, and of many others, are lumped together : here only we obtain the particulars of them. We obtain from the Pipe Rolls the particulars of the great fief of William Peverel, because it was in the king's hands, and that is omitted in this book. In fact, these returns supplement the other, and together make up a more modern account of those fees which, at the time of Domesday, paid scutage to the king. The history of the great baronial family of Ferrars, although in its younger descendants it has produced many peerages, has never been correctly given. This will be attempted in the Parochial portion of the work.

Mr. Llewellynn Jewitt asserts that Henry de Ferrars held 114 manors in Derbyshire alone, and this seems to have been the number of vills he held ; but it appears from the statement of his grandson, William Earl of Derby, that he held this vast estate for the service of sixty knights ; and it would appear that it was for the service of this number, with half a knight's fee added, that he enfeoffed some twenty-six knights during his tenure of the lordship. That (counting the monks of Tutbury, who would find a substitute) was also the number of tenants who are recorded in Domesday. One of these knights answered for the service of five knights ; that is, he was bound to produce them equipped for the field when called upon. Five answered for four each, four answered for three, seven for two, nine for one, and one for half a knight's fee ; 60½ altogether. It is not quite clear how many knights' fees he held in demesne, that is, kept in his own hands ; but, judging roughly, this will give him about fifty manors in hand, for which he paid no hide. For this he would probably be assessed, for the gift of the county; so that he would have no difficulty whatever to form his contingent of the royal army whenever called upon ; and doubtless this is the list of knights, but with few exceptions, who fought under him at the great Battle of the Standards. Comparing the list of his knights as given at Domesday, and that which appears in his great grandson's certificate, it is very difficult to reconcile them ; and yet they must be practically identical, for he only survived two years after Domesday, and he would hardly have changed many tenures in that short period. No doubt the list, as we have it, is the list as it was altered by deaths and successions during the life of his son, that is, during fifty years. But still, every one of these tenants, save those expressly excepted, was a lineal descendant of the Domesday holder, that is of the knight who was enfeoffed by Henry de Ferrars before 1188. It rarely happens that evidence can be obtained of such close approximation to the date of Domesday. The general rule is, that proof can only be obtained of a holding prior to the death of Henry I., nearly fifty years later. This, therefore, is an especial piece of good fortune for the Derbyshire families.

Of course this does not apply to those who, in the time of Earl William, bore a different name. For instance, William de Hastings does not necessarily descend from Henry Cuneigeston or Galfry Marmion from Ivo de Heriz, or William Pantoul from Robert Luvitot, or Henry Hosato from John Turburville, though they may do so through females, or they may have been new grantees. In all the other cases where the property remained in the same name, the identity may be considered fairly and conclusively established, and therefore this follows that the descendants of every one of these knights, with the exception of the four just mentioned, may claim to possess a true Domesday pedigree. Perhaps no other county in England can claim this right for so large a number of families. The

names of the greater part are, as we should expect from the
earl's high position and connections, some of the best known
of the Norman nobility. No less than sixteen of them are
enumerated by Hollinshed in his list collected from the
Chronicles of Normandy, or from that rather suspicious
document, the Roll of Battle Abbey. Suspicious, not because
there is any idea that it is an invention, but because there is
good ground for suspecting that obliging curators of this
document have, from time to time, interpolated certain names
which, no doubt, in the opinion of their descendants, or perhaps
only casual holders, ought to have been there, but which, by
some mysterious accident, were omitted. This may be a libel
upon the Abbey of Battle, but it is a widely spread one. Those
names here given are Baskerville, Curzon, Camera, Curtenei,
Chaucis, Dive, Harcourt, Hastings, Luvitot, Montgomery,
Albini, Nieuton (Neville) fitz Otes, Tuberville, and Trussel,—a
complete chaplet of roses to the genealogist. One thing is
perfectly clear : Henry de Ferrars, whatever he may have done
in keeping English knights or sub-tenants in his own household
and family, so to speak, that is in his own demesne, allowed
but very few of them to be in his service as knights. He
seems to have made an exception in the cases of Swan, of
Cowley, Alric, of Church Somersal, and Cola, and Cole
(probably the same person), who held several manors under
him. But, with these exceptions, we cannot at present
positively identify any others of the names of the Domesday
tenants with those who enjoyed these manors in the time of
Edward the Confessor. True, twenty years had passed away—
nearly a generation, perhaps quite one in those days of conquest and plunder during the first twenty years of William's
reign, when many an English head was prematurely laid low.

It is difficult positively to identify the tenants under Edward
the Confessor, but the Domesday scribe, no doubt instigated by
the Domesday Commissioner, the Earl himself, has given them
with more exactness than we generally obtain, and we are able
to identify amongst the tenants several Royal Princes. Siward
the Earl, Edwin, his brother, Earl Walleof, Godwin, Leuric,
and Levenot (younger Princes), and as we should expect from
such company, many great Danish names, so that it is
probable that there would be fewer changes in the tenancies

than at first sight appears ; but these questions will more
properly be discussed in the separate portions of the parochial
history.   At present it is sufficient to call attention to the
jewels with which Domesday is thickly studded, and in no
part of England more richly than in this half county of Derby.
Evidently from the great beauty and charms of its situa-
tion, valuable for its mining facilities, enjoyable for its sport,
it was a favourite spot for Royalty, and would lose none
of its attractiveness in the hands of its princely lord, who,
perhaps not unlike some of his great successors, knew well
how to combine the pleasures and hospitalities, the true
charms of life, with a due regard to its duties and profits—
a good guarantee for a permanent settlement, and far more
admirable than the lavish splendour, with the inevitable
ignominy to follow, of the unhappy spendthrift.

The old Earls of Derby were proud of their connection
with mining industries, and not only assumed the character
in their titles, but emblazoned it upon their arms.   The
horseshoes borne by these princes were no unmeaning insignia ;
it was an exposition of the fact that the shoeing of horses and
the winning and preparing the metal for the purpose was
their business.   In that age of blood and iron, as in our
own, the man who could gather his wealth from the bowels
of the earth was not to be despised or trodden under
foot, and he held his own with the mightiest in the land,
a happy safeguard for peaceful industry and honourable
enterprise.

An alphabetical list of the tenants of Henry de Ferrars,
collected from Domesday, is already published at page 74 of
Section I.   In this return they will be taken in the order given
by the Earl himself in his certificate.   There is a very remarkable feature in this return which gives it an exceptional and
great value.   The Earl William has divided his return, not
according to the tenor of the King's writ, which directed him
simply to say which were of the old and which of the new
feoffment, but as before noticed he has divided his return into
no less than four divisions, the first and most valuable being
those knights with their precedessors who were enfeoffed by
his great grandfather, who died in 1088, the next list those
who were enfeoffed by his grandfather, who died in 1138, and

then those by his father, who was probably only just dead, and who died in 1162.

In these certificates unfortunately, though we get the full name of the tenant, we do not learn the names of their fees, whilst Domesday gives the contrary information, a good account of the fee, but only as a rule the Christian names of the tenants, and not always that, but the return of Henry Ferrars supplies an account of the tenants at these different epochs, and in some places giving a complete pedigree from Domesday, in the majority of cases taking us back within two years of its date.

The few facts relating to the motive of these returns, which are to be found in the Derbyshire portion of the book, are very much condensed compared to those of some other counties, but an examination of a considerable portion of the whole returns has failed to produce any satisfactory evidence which might determine their date and meaning. In no instance has a full copy of the King's writ been discovered, but in several there is a recital of it, which probably gives the best part of it, notably is this the case in the return of Robert de Brinton, of Staffordshire. He writes to the King—" I, Robert de Brinton, myself, and others, my peers (comparibus meis), are directed by your letter that by the fidelity and allegiance which we owe to you our Lord by our letters under seal, we should show to you what knights we have of the old feoffment of the time of the King your grandfather, and what knights we have of the new feoffment after the time of Henry your grandfather, and what of our own demesne."

Herbert de Castell, in the County of Salop, began in the same form. Scores of returns show that the King's order was strictly to divide the returns of the knights into the two classes of new and old feoffments, and these recitals place beyond all doubt what was the King's definition of each of these classes. Supplement this by the fact that throughout these returns the reign of Stephen and his very name is ignored, although an occasional reference is made to his period as the time of war, and we obtain an important clue to guide us in the search.

In Cambridgeshire, Mannassah Damartin stated that he held one fee in the time of King Henry, and that in the time of the war he gave Walter de Gornac one quarter of it, which

William, his son, then held, and, he added, that of new feoffment he had none. The mode by which the return is made is significant. John de Port, in Southampton, writes the King— "Because on your part you have commanded that I should certainly make you to know what of old and what of new feoffment belongs to me (respicet) quoad yourself what and which fees I hold. By this present writing I truly state."

Other Barons show that they made the enquiry by jury of legal and honest men. The Bishop of Bath made his return by his legal knights, and offered to give further information if required. Earl Patric (Salisbury) made the return by his honest and ancient men. Probably the universal method was to obtain the return by such a jury, and the sole privilege which was originally proposed to be given was, that the machinery of the baronial court was not to be superseded, by the king's justices : a great advantage to the lord, since it carried with it the power of selecting the jury.

The return for the Earl of Arundel's Sussex fee shows that it, probably like the rest, was made upon oath. This was an exceptional case, for it would appear that this barony was then in the king's hands; and it is recited that King Henry, on account of certain contentions which arose between the knights of the Honour of Arundel concerning service in the army of Wales, chose four knights of the highest rank of the said Honour—Ranulf de Sartil, Ralf fil Bruer, Will de Favarches, and Peter de Hatton, and made them acknowledge the services of the Honour, and therefore no one dare be heard against their legality and oath.

Richard de Aquila declared that he had made no new feoffment in Sussex since the reign of Henry I. John Count of Ewe declared he had fifty-six fees of the feoffment of the time of King Henry I., and no fees of new feoffment.

And this seemed the real point of the return, to show if any feoffments had been made *tempe* Stephen, and by whom.

Walter de Med, in Kent, was probably caught, for he returned to " Henry by the grace of God, King of the Angles. May it be known to you that in the year and day in which King Henry, your grandfather, was alive and dead, Galf Talbot held twenty knights' fees of him, which, by your favour, I now hold of you."

Walter fil Helte, in the same county, had to return that he had only three knights' fees (no date of feoffment given?) but after the death of Henry the king, I gave one-fifth of a fee of my own demesne to a certain one of my family. As no consent of the king is mentioned, this was probably done in the time of King Stephen.

Richard de Greenstead, in Wilts., answered that he had no knights of the new or old feoffment, but for his demesne he did the service of one knight to the king.

So William de London, in the same county, by his return admitted that he ought to answer for his fee by the services of his body.

In Somerset, Alexander de Alno declared that he had enfeoffed no one since the death of Henry I., but that his father had given to his brother Hugo, the knight, certain lands, but this was in the time of King William.

In the same county Hugo de Curcel (the probable ancestor of the Ducal House of Marlboro') stated that he held of the king one knight's fee, and that his father gave one quarter of it to Roger de Granton. This scion of the House of Churchill was apparently, like some of the others, making an evasive return, but this must not be rashly concluded, because if these returns are of different dates, as it seems quite certain that they are, only some of them were made on Henry's accession, and after that period the distinction of new and old feoffment became of less importance, and might not be insisted upon or noticed.

Wm. de Moun (Somerset) returned the knights enfeoffed from the time of King Henry I.; Wm. de Curci Dapifer those which his grandfather, his father, and himself held, just as did the Earl of Ferrars in his return; so Humphrey de Bohun gave the fees of which his grandfather was enfeoffed of the first feoffment. These returns appear to have been made at a later date than Henry's accession, as in fact we know to be the case in the return of William de Ferrars, Earl of Derby, for he did not obtain seizin in the sixth year of Henry the king, the year his father died, for the lands were then in the king's hands, though he certainly had seizin on the 14th of the king. Sometimes two knights made a joint return, as in the case of Robert Peverel and Norman de Normanville, who held one knight's fee of the king in Sussex, Robert doing service for two parts, Norman for the other.

The Bishop of Exeter returned under his writ sealed and aptum : proof that these charters were made in the most solemn and complete manner.

The returns made by those who divided the feoffments by the epochs of their ancestors, would seem to indicate that their certificates had been preserved, and were, in fact, being recited, so that we seem to possess, in some instances in substance, the very certificates of those ancestors ; and the later returns of the Testa de Nevil proves that this system of making certificates of knights' fees existed for centuries afterwards. It was evidently therefore by some accident, such as that already suggested, that they were collected and transcribed in this book.

The following notes are taken almost haphazard from many sources, which will be more regularly arranged hereafter. They must be taken as merely tentative in some cases, and in none as exhaustive. They are given to show the bent of the author's mind, but it must be taken that they are all open to correction, and many of them, doubtless, will be corrected hereafter. As a rule, those families only whose histories are in doubt, are at present noticed.

CHAPTER IV.

***

The Certificate of the Earl of Ferrars.

***

No I.—THE CHARTER OF WILLIAM, EARL DE FERRARS (c. 1162).

Henry King of England, to his well-beloved baron William Earl de Ferrars' health. We command you that . . . . . in the time of King Henry, our grandfather . . . .

1 AND 2. — HENRY FIL SEWELL (SASWALDI) HELD FIVE KNIGHTS' FEES, FULCHER, HIS BROTHER, FOUR, AND NOW (1162) THE HEIRS OF SASWALDI HOLD NINE FEES TOGETHER.

NOTE.—At Domesday Sasuallo held Hoge, Hatune, and Etewall. Testa de N.: Sewell fil Henry held Hoka (qy. Hoga).

This is a curious statement, from which it would seem that both, or at any rate one, of these knights had died without leaving issue, for the same heirs represented both, and from the fact that the name of the heirs were unmentioned, it is probable that they were co-parceners, and female heirs or their descendants, and that as yet no partition had been made between them, so that no one was as yet responsible for the services due from the fees. Henry fil Sewalon was living at the time of the first Pipe Roll, for there he is entered as accounting for seven marcs of silver that he might be quit, *i.e.*, released from his oath.

This is a most interesting pedigree, and several families claim descent, but it is to be feared that their claims will not stand the brunt of investigation, for their only proof seems to be that their ancestors bore the names of some of the manors held by Saswalo, which is simply idle. The family of Shirlev especially seem at fault with their proof, and they do not even possess the advantage of possessing any of Sewel's manors. The heralds differ amongst themselves as to the history of the Shirley family. When this is the case, it is almost more dangerous than when they are in agreement, though that is bad enough. But if they differ, it is tolerably certain that one of the body has gone wrong somewhere, and very wrong too, if his fellows will not support him. That the family of Sewell were the chief tenants of the Earl de Ferrars in the reign of Stephen or Henry II., is clear from a charter of Robert, grandson of Henry Ferrars, concerning Leke, in which Hugh fil Sewell is the chief witness, and Henry fil Sewal also attested it (1138-62). Some authorities state that Henry and Fulcher had three other brethren, and, if this can be shown positively, there may be hope of proving the pedigree.

The surname of Sewell remained long in Derbyshire. It is to be found in a list of knights' fees of 10 Henry VI., when John Sewale held land in Wirksworth; and the name of Swale is to be found in Hardwick charters of the same period. So, too, at an earlier period it appears in some Osberton charters. Domesday only indicates three of the manors held by this family, and it may be difficult to recover the rest. They then held Hoon, Hatton, and Etwall.

Sewell fil Fulcher (who may or may not be of the same family: both Fulc and Sewell are common Christian names), gave Aldwark to Derley Abbey, a manor which was Ferrars', but was probably appurtinent to Bradburn, held by de Cauz. He is mentioned in a Pipe Roll of 21 Henry II. A Henry fil Fulcher is mentioned in the same Pipe Roll, and in 15 Henry II.; and a Robert fitz Fulc in 26 Henry II. In 7 John, Henry fil Sewall sued Sarra de Hedesferes and William de London. Sewall fitz Henry, 1202, fined, with William de Stretton concerning one bovate of land in Barlborough, and the descendants of a collateral branch of this family may be traced long afterwards.

This brings down .the family to the period when territorial surnames were adopted, and it is to be hoped that such a transmutation of names may be discovered.

It is difficult to determine the nationality of the sons of Saswald, or Saswalo, from the name. Henry and ˙Fule are both Norman names, but they were so commonly Norse, that they were plentiful wherever the Danes settled ; and these names may have been given in gratitude to the Earl de Ferrars for placing this knight in so high a position as chief tenant of the Honour. The strong probability is, that he was a relation of his lord, possibly a son-in-law, or grandson, as was the case with the next tenant.

3.—WILLIAM FIL NIGEL HELD FOUR KNIGHTS' FEES ; NOW ROBERT, HIS SON, HOLDS THEM.

NOTE.—There is no doubt about one at least of the manors (Catton) held by this knight, nor any about his indentity, for Domesday records that he held Catton (Chetune), and the Baron St. Amand obtained it as one of the co-heirs of Robert fil Nigel, Lord of Cainhoe.

The Abingdon cartulary shows that in 1107 Henry Albini of Cainhoe, whose mother was Amicia, daughter of Henry de Ferrars, had a younger brother, William. There is probably some error in the generally received pedigree of the Albinis of Cainhoe, for it has to be explained how the older branch of the family came to inherit this, if William fil Nigel was the younger brother of Henry, for it is generally recorded that Robert was his eldest son, and that he was followed by another Robert, whose co-heir Ailmer St. Amand married, and the difficulty is the greater that a family of Albini remained in Derby for centuries after this date, who held Abney of the Ferrars family. One of this family attested Robert de Ferrars' charter, 1138-62, concerning Leke. Robert fitz Nigel was one of Henry de Ferrars' Staffordshire knights. The proof that the names Abney and Albini are identical is simply overwhelming, and inasmuch as this name was well known at Domesday, it seems

20

impossible that the manor of Abney can be identified with Habenai of Domesday, as both Lysons and Glover insist. Swain held it àt Domesday under William Peverel, under whom it is not recorded that the Albinis held land.   They held Uffington, in South Wingfield, and Pentric under Ralf fitz Hubert, but that was to be expected, seeing the close connection of their families.   For a full account of the Albinis the learned reader is referred to the author's history of the House of Arundel.   The Abneys of Willesley now undoubtedly represent the Derbyshire branch of this great family, who are of the male blood of the family of the ducal house of Normandy, the Lord of St. Sauveur, the ancestor of the Albinis, Earls of Arundel (and the Lords of Cainhoe and Belvoir), being the next heir male to the duchy upon the death of Duke Robert in 1035.   The Duke of Norfolk now represents the Earls of Arundel.

A William fil Nigel held Caldwell, of Burton Abbey, at a very early period.   Dr. Cox suggests that he was de Gresley. This may be so, but at this period the Gresleys were not certainly tenants of the Ferrars' family.   It is clear that they were knights of the Honour of Peverel, and would not become knights of this honour until, in the turbulent period of King John's reign (if any particular portion of it can be so styled), William de Ferrars intruded into the Peverel inheritance.

In 23 Henry II., Robert de Albini rendered composition of five marcs for the duel of the Earl de Ferrars; that is, he was one of his sureties; and then headed the list of his knights (see page 121, where the names of a number of the earl's tenants of that date are to be found.)

4.—RICHARD DE CURZON HELD FOUR KNIGHTS' FEES; ROBERT, HIS SON, NOW HOLDS THEM.

Gilbert held Chelardestune at Domesday.

NOTE.—Robert de Curzon held Ketelston for half a knight's fee and one fee in Twyford, and Thomas de Curzon held four parts of a knight's fee, in Ketleston.   Test. de Nev.

The very greatest interest attaches to this pedigree.   In point of antiquity, coupled with the uniform high position held by the family through all generations from the time of the Con-quest, it is almost the premier pedigree of the county.

Genealogists have meddled with this pedigree only to mar it, and that which has been detailed by the heralds in their visitations abounds with errors, but nothing can destroy its absolute integrity as an undoubted Domesday pedigree, the family having always enjoyed the same manors from father to son to the present time. The heralds persist in deriving the family from Roger, who held Croxall at Domesday, alleging that the Croxall branch is the elder. This, however, appears extremely doubtful, for that manor clearly came into the family by the marriage of Rich de Curzon with Petronilla, the daughter and heiress (or co-heir) of Walter de Camville, who was probably the descendant of Roger of Domesday. There are two manors which the Curzons possess, of the origin of which (out of all their manors) we have no account. These are Kedleston and Weston Underwood. It is tolerably clear that they formed the whole or part of the lesser barony of Richard de Curzon at the time when he married the heiress of Camville, and at Domesday, both of them were held by one Guilbert, who, in all probability, was the true ancestor of the family. A Curzon held these estates in 1088; only two years previously Guilbert held them, therefore it may be con-tended he was the common ancestor of the family. It is to be hoped, however, as before observed, that further research will make this quite clear.

The certificate of the Earl de Ferrars places the presumption of a descent from the Domesday lord infinitely higher than that which can generally be drawn from these documents, since it reduces the ordinary space of seventy-five years to two, in fact, to so high a probability that it is almost a certainty.

23 Henry II. Robert de Curzon rendered composition of 40s. on account of the duel of the earl.

5.—WALTER DE MONTGOMERY HELD FOUR KNIGHTS' FEES.

NOTE.—Testa de Nevil, Wm. de Montgomery held Marston and Cubberley for three fees and one-tenth and one-thirteenth. The Book of Aids shows that this family then held land in

Marchington, Cuberley, Sudbury, Aston, Snelleston, Eyton, Sedgeshall, Orlaston, and Sonsal. This is, again, one of the grandest pedigrees in Derbyshire; but, unlike the family of Curzon, they no longer remain (at least under that name) in this county. The representation of the family is presumably with the families of Stanhope, the elder co-heir, and the only one who left issue ultimately surviving, having married Sir John Port, of Etwall, whose daughter and heiress, Margaret, married Sir Thomas Stanhope, of Shelford, ancestor of the Earls of Chesterfield, the Earls of Harrington, and the Earls of Stanhope. It is difficult, however, to state positively who is now the true representative of the family, so many of the Earls of Chesterfield having died without issue, or leaving only female issue, the first of whom, in point of seniority, being of course the true representative of the Montgomerys.

The Vernons of Sudbury, although they possess several of the manors of the Montgomerys, have in fact no descent from them. Sir John Vernon of Haddon married one of the co-heirs of Sir John Montgomery in the reign of Henry VIII., but his issue ultimately became extinct, and his estates passed under his will to the issue of an elder brother of Sir John Vernon, from whom the present Lord Vernon descends. Although there cannot be a doubt that the Montgomerys were Domesday tenants of the Ferrars, yet just as in the case with the Curzons, the Domesday ancestor is uncertain. The probabilities seem to lie between Ralf and John, the latter of whom is generally supposed to be the true ancestor. This interesting question must await solution until the history of the several manors held by this family have been more carefully enquired into. The arms of this family would seem to indicate a descent from the family of Albini, since it is a derivative coat of that of Ivri or Evroux, which Wm. Albini, Earl of Arundel, of this house, bore prior to the acquisition of that earldom.

One of the Domesday tenants of the Ferrars called John was probably de Harcourt, who subsequently changed his name to that of Heris. He was nearly related to Roger Montgomery, being descended from Herfast, the brother of the Duchess Gunnor, amongst whose descendants we find Earl Roger de Montgomery. Amongst his knights there was a Ralf de Montgomery, who was possibly the Lord of Snelston and

Cubley. Certainly the latter place was a part of the barony of this family. For a full account of the family of Montgomery, the author must refer the reader to his history of the House of Arundel.

Walter de Montgomery attested a charter to Alan de Leke, nephew of Elfnot, concerning that manor 1138-62.

1175 Walter Montgomery paid 40s. on account of the earl's duel.

6.—ROBERT DE BAKEPUZ HELD FOUR KNIGHTS'

FEES.

NOTE.—Testa de Nevil proves that Galfry de Bakepuz held Alkmanton for 3 parts of 1 knight's fee, and that John de Bakepuz held Barton for 1 fee. Both these manors were held at Domesday by Ralf, doubtless their ancestor. In all probabiiity the Earl de Ferrars had more than one knight named Ralf. The Book of Aids shows that John de Bakepuz then held 3 parts of a fee in Alkmanton and Barton, formerly held by Robert Bakepuz.

This family were long resident in the county of Derby, certainly much later than the reign of Edward I., which date Lysons gives for the termination of their residence.

In the time of Earl Henry, ante 1088, they held more manors, but their descendants were resident in some of these as late, and probably later, than the reign of King Henry VI., although doubtless their chief property had passed to the Blounts.

Besides the high position they bore amongst the lesser barons of the chief barony, their coat armour suggests a family relationship, for, in addition to the ancient arms of Ivri, which they probably obtained from the Albinis, they bore the three horse-shoes of their chief, which they would not assume unless there was affinity of blood as well as a feudal relationship.

1138-62. Geoffry de Bakepuz attested a charter of Earl Robert de Ferrars.

Henry II. Walter de Bakepuz attested the charter of Welbeck Abbey.

1167. Walter and John de Bakepuz were sureties for their lord.

1197. Robert de Bakepuz fined with the Abbot of Derley and the Knights' Hospitallers concerning the church of Barew.

1235. Walter de Bakepuz and Elizabeth, his wife, at Blythe.

33 Henry III. Geoffry de Bakepuz and Eincynea, his wife, held land in Nettlesworth by knight service of Malvesinus de Herecy and Theophania, his wife, and they of the Honour of Tickhill. This estate eventually came to the family of Denman, ancestors of the Lords Denman, in descent from Herecys.

Sir Galf de Bakepuz and Amicia, his wife, granted land to Lenton Priory (Register 137).

C. Edward I. Ralf de Bakepuz (Subsidy Roll).

20 Edward III. John fil John de Bakepuz (Book of Aids).

25-33 Edward III. Thomas Bakepuz (Subsidy Roll).

6 Henry VI. James Bakepuz of Alkmanton, and John of Barton (Subsidy Rolls).

10 Henry VI. Wm. Bakepuz, of London, held land in Derbyshire.

7.—BASKERVILLE, HENRY DE, AND THEN JOHN, HIS SON, HELD THREE KNIGHTS' FEES.

NOTE.—This name seems to be another form of that of Boscherville.

1266. Sir John Baskerville obtained a grant of Old Whittington, in Cheshire, from Robert de Camville.

8.—ROBERT FIL WALKELIN, AND NOW ROBERT, HIS SON, HELD TWO KNIGHTS' FEES.

NOTE.—There is but little doubt that in this knight we have a relation of the earl in the male line, the surname fitz Walkelin being that by which many of his family were known. In the face of the fact that the pedigree of Ferrars has never been satisfactorily worked out, it is dangerous to speculate as to the exact relationship, but, seeing that we obtain here three generations, the probability is that Robert fitz Walkelin, who was enfeoffed by Henry de Ferrars ante 1088, was his brother.

Robert, uncle of the earl, who was surety for him in 1175, was probably this tenant. The word avunculus, by which the relationship is described, is a very loose one, and is wide enough to include the descendants of the uncles and aunts of a person on either side, though at one time it is supposed to have included only those relations by the mother's side,—in fact it has little less meaning than the word kinsman, or cousin.

The Burton Cartulary shows that in 1150-59 Abbot Robert granted to Robert fil Robert fil Walkelin (no doubt this knight) certain land in Heanor, to be held of the Abbey at the nominal rent of half a mark. Gaufridus Abbot (1114-50) having granted to him other land in Oure at 5s. rent. The same abbot granted to Robert de Ferrars, at a rent of 5s., certain land in Tickenhall, which his father had previously held, for which he was bound to protect the Abbey.

Dr. Cox appears to identify these two knights.

The account of the fitz Walkelins will occupy much space in the Parochial History.

9.—ROBERT DE DUNE, AND THEN JAMES, HIS SON, HELD TWO KNIGHTS' FEES.

NOTE.—Testa de Nevil shows that Robert de Dun held 2 fees in Breydeston.

It is probable that these fees lay in Breadsal and Dalbury. Robert de Dun was Lord of Dalbury *tempe* Henry II. (Dugdale's Monasticon 1, 355, first edition.)

At Domesday Dalbury is described as a hamlet of Mickleover, which was then belonging to the Abbot of Burton.

This family remained in the service of the Earls de Ferrars for several generations. The manor of Breadsal, which they held, came to the Curzons through the marriage of an heiress, but the younger branches of the family long remained in the county.

In 31 Henry III. (Rolls called Tower Records, but properly forming part of the Coram Rege and Assize Rolls) there was an assize to enquire whether Sampson le Dun and Galf de Skefington had disseized Robert de Ferrars (meaning the earl) of 15 tofts, 2 carucates, and 24 bovates, 2 mills and 4 acres of wood, and 1s. and one pound pepper rent in Breadsal, which he claimed to hold of the feoffment of Jacobus de Audeley.

Sampson said that the earl commanded him that he should send to him his palfry, which was a fine one, and when he was unwilling to send it the earl sent his knights to the town of Breadsal, who, by the writ of the same earl, seized it and took it to a certain hermitage, and the same earl held it in hand for a long time, and afterwards gave it to Robert de Stradley, who gave it to Hugo de Dun, with Nicolas de Marnham, the earl's senescal.

The earl asserted that Sampson had subsequently surrendered to him.

The same year (same Roll) Wm. de Sauneby and Sibella, his wife, widow of Robert de Dun, sued Henry de Dun for a certain rent from Breadsal, and Sampson de Dun for another rent, who called Margaret, fil and heir of Roger fil Robert de Dun, to warranty, who was an infant within age in the custody of Hugo de Meynil.

The Duns remained many generations as landed proprietors in this county.

10.—RALF PARVUS HELD TWO KNIGHTS' FEES WHICH REGINALD DE GRESLEY THEN HELD.

Testa de Nevil shows that Wm. de Gresley and Gilbert de Seagrave held three parts of one fee in Linton. The connection between this de Gresley and the family of Drakelow has not yet been discovered. It was not until about the year 1200 that the latter family became knights of the Earl of Ferrars; but in 1178, Robert and Henry de Gresley, no doubt of this family, were sureties for the earl.

The Liber Niger shows that Robert de Gresley held three fees in Staffordshire of Robert de Stafford, which at Domesday were held by Nigel, and it is assumed, perhaps, without sufficient proof, that he was the direct ancestor.

Kirkby's Quest shows that Galf de Gresley held three fees in the reign of Edward I., and the Book of Aids (20 Edward IV.) that one fee in Lothington had descended to John, his son.

The Gresley pedigree, like so many others, has been built up upon assumptions, the truth of which it will be attempted hereafter to test.

11.—ROBERT DE LUVITOT, AND THEN WILLIAM PANTOUL, HELD TWO FEES FOR THE SERVICE OF ONE KNIGHT.

Wm. Earl Ferrars by charter now at Hardwick Hall, granted and confirmed to Maurice, nephew (nepos) of Robert de Luvitot, the manor of Wodham, which Robert Earl Ferrars, his father gave to him to hold in inheritance in exchange for his uncle's lands given to Wm. Pantoul.

General Wrottesley has assumed the meaning of returns in this form to be, that the tenant last named is the under-tenant of the former, but this charter seems to solve the difficulty, for here, at any rate, there was no undertenancy, but a simple exchange. The difficulty is to understand the difference of an old feoffment of this kind, and a new grant or feoffment. Perhaps it is that the new tenant, by arrangement, succeeds to the whole obligations and duties of the old one, as heir.

This grant was made by the earl in his court before himself, his barons and knights, a grand list, which is of great value, since so little is recorded of this barony.

They were Richard, Abbot of St. Peter's, sur Dive Fulc, Prior of Tutbury, Roger Chaplain of the Earl H. fil Fulc (Sewall), and H. Dankerville, Will Cap. Maurice and Anst. clerics, William de Ferr and Hugo, brothers of the Earl, Robert and H. his uncles; William Pantoul, Robert de Piri (Dapifer), Robert fil Walkelin, and H. his brother, and Peter and Walter de Montgomery, and Ralf his son, and Rad de Montgomery, and William fitz Herbert, and Walter de Somerville, and Adam de Stanton, and William his brother, and Humphrey de Tolka Rad de Boscerville and Renald de G(ou)sel, Harald de Lek and Alan his son, Thomas Venator of the Earl, and Robert de C(ur)cun, and Rad de M(u)st(ers). H. de Cavis, and William de Dun, and Robert fil Ralf, and Peter de Sandiacre, and William de Munjoia, Robt. Pincerna and Thos. de Piri, Galf de Camara and John de Boscervill, G. de Bak, Rann de Manville and German his brother, John de Bak, Wido de Rochford, Richard fil Alan and Reginald de Danesia, Laurence and Ralf de Torp, and Gaufry and Gilbert his sons, H. fil Robert de Lega, Robert fil Richard de Normanton, Wm. de Coddinc, and Robert and Ralf his brothers, and Wm. fil Alcher and G. his son, Richard fitz Herbert, and Alan fitz John, and Roger Galum.

12.—HENRY DE CAMBRIES HELD ONE KNIGHT'S FEE.

NOTE.—Testa de Nevil shows that Henry de Chaumbreys held half a fee in Brunaveston. The manors of - Barocote and Burnaston were held by Roger fil Walter de Cambries in 1290, and it seems that they were the manors held by this knight, in 1088, one Henry, who is presumably the same, holding them at Domesday, and of the same knight, also Norbury. If this be so, it would seem doubtful if he were not another member of the Ferrars' family, for Robert fil Henry de Ferrars gave Norbury to Tutbury early in the reign of Henry I., and the Prior, in 1126, gave it to William fitz Herbert, probably identical with his nephew of that name, in fee farm at 100s. rent. He was ancestor of the family of Fitzherbert of Tissington.

13.—WILLIAM DE SEYLE, AND THEN RALF, HIS SON, HELD TWO KNIGHTS' FEES.

NOTE.—Lysons gives no account of this knight, but it would seem, from the Burton Cartulary, that Ralf, the son, was constable of the Earl Robert (fo. 33).

28th November, 1208, a Lucian de Seille, and Agatha his wife, fined, with Bertram de Caldun, and Alice his wife, con cerning a wood in Herteshorn, called Danewellhai. Amicia de Albini sued Lucian fil Robert de Seille for land there, to which he had ingress only through Lucian his grandfather. Lucian, the grandson, called to warranty John fitz Herbert, who could not come, because he was in the king's service abroad, and, in fact, a prisoner of the King of France in the castle of Baalan.

14.—GALF DE CAMARA HELD TWO FEES, OF WHICH ROBERT FIL RALF AND PETER DE GOLDINGTON THEN EACH HELD ONE.

NOTE.—This again raises the difficulty mooted by General Wrottesly, and this is complicated by a similar entry being found in the Staffordshire account (which the General has published, though without notice of this entry). There Geoffry de Camara held 2 fees of Henry de Ferrars, which the General identifies as in Marchinton, which the same two knights then held.

If their estates were held officially, or rather for official services connected with the county, it would almost seem as if this Robert fil Ranulf was the sheriff, and Peter de Goldington his under-sheriff, for both held certain offices in connection with the treasury of the county, as is evinced by many entries in the Pipe Rolls, from the 11th to the 14th year of Henry II.

15.—YVO DE HARECOURT AND WILLIAM FIL WALKELIN HELD THREE KNIGHTS' FEES, WHICH THE HEIRS OF GALFR MARMION THEN HELD.

NOTE.—This is a very puzzling entry, and it is difficult to understand how two men, being owners of the same knight's fees near Domesday, except by sale, could pass their interest by descent to the same man, unless at the first period they represented co-heirs, and one of them died without issue. In the year 1100 or 1102, Robert de Heriz held Edensor, probably of Henry de Ferrars, for it was his at Domesday; and he held Oxcroft of William Peverel, for he made grants out of both of them to his foundation at Lenton about that date. We have no history of Oxcroft from Lysons. He merely mentions that Heriz held it *tempe* Henry III., and in his account of Edensor he does not refer to the Heriz family. Now Robert held this latter place, as well as Wingfield, at Domesday; and he is presumably the Robert de Heriz of fifteen years later. He left a son, Ivo, it is very certain, for he appears from the first Roll of the Pipe to have been sheriff, or perhaps farmer, of the county at some earlier period, and he then accounts for a

payment for his land at Wilgeby, where, at Domesday, William
Peverel held two bovates and a half of Clifton Sok, and which,
very clearly, Robert de Heriz held in the latter part of the
reign of King Henry II. In 26 Henry II., Adeliza, the widow
of William de Heriz, the elder brother of Robert (whose heir
he was), fined with the king that she should not be compelled
to marry. In the reign of Henry III., Ivo de Heriz, son of
Robert, held Oxcroft, Wyngfield, and Lyvechief, for two
knights' fees. If this family are identical with that of Yvo,
the knight of 1088, it is clear that they must descend from a
younger branch of it. Of this William fil Walkelin, nothing
seems to be known. Possibly he was another brother of Henry
de Ferrars, and he probably died without heirs; though how
the heirs of Galfry de Marmion succeeded to the inheritance,
whether by descent or purchase, is unknown. Nor is it clear
who these heirs were. One of them was probably Albreda,
the wife of William de Camville, of Clifton Childcot, in
Staffordshire, who 9 John sued William de Berkley concerning
Childcot in Derbyshire, which was soc to it.

There is a very puzzling account of a fitz Walkelin family,
of Derby, which possibly may be the same. In the reign o
Henry II., Walkelin of Derby, and Goda his wife, were dealing
with certain rights in a mill at Derby, which he had purchased
of William de Heriz. Was this William that son of Ivo de
Heriz who died 23rd Henry II.? Magister Robert fil Goda,
who died ante 1176, granted a messuage, with a bakery
(cum furno), which Wachelin held in Derby, and the land
which Petronilla fil Peter (his father) gave to the Canons of
Derley. It would seem that he had several younger brothers
called Wachiline, Henry, Augustine, Peter, William, and Walter.
Most of them Ferrars names, and curiously a Wachiline de
Ferrars, an uncle of William the Earl, married, presumably in
the time of Stephen or of Henry I., one Goda, the daughter
of Robert Todeni, with whom it seems tempting to identify
this couple. But the Ferrars' pedigree is in such an uncertain
state as to dates, and they have adhered so frequently to the
same Christian names, that it is by no means safe to trust to
the printed accounts.

16.—RICHARD DE FIFEHED HELD TWO FEES.

17.—WM. DE BOSKERVILLE HELD 3 KNIGHTS' FEES, OF WHICH RALF HIS SON HELD ONE, ODO FITZ JOHN HELD ANOTHER, AND ROBERT (II.), EARL DE FERRARS (1162), GAVE THE THIRD TO THE KNIGHT TEMPLARS.

NOTE.—Robert de Boskerville held Eisse, Hiltune, and Turvedestun at Domesday.

The question arises who was this William de Boskerville, and Derbyshire historians give no answer to it. We must in this case go direct to Norman records for an answer, and we at once see that Boscheville in Normandy, or part of it, was the territory of the Avenel family, another great Derbyshire family of whom as little is known. Now nothing is clearer than that the Avenel family held Haddon at a very early period, for the foundation charter of Lenton, c. 1101, was attested by Avenel of Haddon, and he granted land out of Haddon, Method-we-ploth, and Maniax to that foundation; and Wm. Avenel, who in all probability was this Wm. de Boskerville, attested a somewhat later charter of the son of the founder (after 1113).

Robert de Avenel attested the foundation charter of Welbec in the time of Stephen, and Ralf de Avenel, early in King Henry II.'s reign, gave the church of Sutton to the Prior of Trentham. (Madox Form, Ang., No. 4. 507.)

1175. Ralf de Boscherville was surety half a mark on account of the Earl's duel.

We obtain no trace of Wm. Avenel in Domesday, but we learn that at Domesday Haddon was part of the ancient demesne of the Crown, as was Oneis, another of Wm. Avenel's manors, except one carucate in Haddon which Henry de Ferrars claimed against the king. These Berewites, with others, belonged to Bakewell, where there was a lead work, which with the king's other mining districts were now in the hands of the Baron's Fossiers, and long held by them, till the favoured family of the Gernons, the alleged ancestors of the Dukes of Devonshire, possessed it. Certainly we gain from this no direct evidence of a holding under Henry de Ferrars. We must look, therefore, to see if any evidence is procurable from other records, and fortunately we shall obtain from the partition of his estates in the time of King Richard an account of the fees which were then held by the family, and which were divided between the co-heirs, Simon Basset and Helizabeth his wife, and Richard Vernon and Amicia his wife.

The Rotuli Curiæ Regis, No. 5, which was formerly dated by the authorities of the Record Office as that of the second year of King John, but upon the redating, which was made in consequence of the author's strictures (written in several articles of the "Law Review" of 1875), is now dated 6 Richard I. Now, beside the fact that some of the Rolls of this bundle are of the date of King Henry III., this date can hardly be correct, since the Pipe Roll of that year shows that . . . Basset paid 100 shillings for half the farm of Bassellaw. A Richard de Vernon farmed the other half, and the same roll shows that at the same date Hugh de Haddon (who was probably a Basset) paid £10 for having his land, which was a knight's fee, in Haddon. (We must remember that there are two Haddons.) More than this, the Sheriff accounts for 12s., the value of the goods sold this year, late of Robert de Avenel, "one of the king's enemies," from which fact it is easy to read that Robert de Avenel had for some reason forfeited his lands, and that they were in the king's hands, yet his co-heirs were practically allowed to enjoy them, paying a rent, or farming them from the Crown. The meaning of this can probably be ascertained from a charter now at Belvoir Castle (where many valuable Vernon papers are deposited by reason of the representation of the Dukes of Rutland of this branch of the Vernon family.) The charter is of William Avenel, and it concedes to Richard Vernon and Simon Basset, who had married his two daughters and co-heirs, all his estate in free marriage.

The partition, of whatever date it is, shows that Simon Basset obtained the whole vill of Haddon and half of Basselaw, whilst Richard de Vernon obtained Hadstock, Hurlingburc, and half of Basselaw.

The Croxton Chartulary, also at Belvoir, shows that Gilbert Avenel was a benefactor granting land in Empton. This Gilbert was clearly in the direct Haddon line.

The Pipe Rolls for Notts. and Derby give some evidence.

2 Henry II. Gervase Avenel paid 20 marks for the land of Basselaw.

19 Henry II. Gervase and Robert Avenel were two of the overseers respecting works done to the Castles of Bolsover and Peck.

Robert again in 20 Henry II., Gervase in 23 Henry II.

In 26 Henry II., the sheriff accounted for 68s. for corn sold off the land of Gervase Avenel of the Honour of Peverel, proof that he had forfeited his lands, unless they were for other reason, perhaps, a minority, then in the king's hands.

In 7 Richard I., Wm. Basset was charged 40 marcs for land ih Nottingham and Derby, and Robert Avenel one marc for seven shillings rent in Pleslie and in Sutton.

In 3 John, Wm. Avenel paid 4 marcs for having writ to recover one fee in Basselaw, Bubbeshill, Cardeburc, and Froggat, against Simon Basset, and Richard de Vernon and Alice his wife. Unfortunately, we can find no trace of this suit in the Rot. Cur. Regis, so that the real reason of the disappearance of the Avenels is not clear.

In 6 Richard I., Amicia ux Gilbert Avenel placed her husband against Mathew fil Odo (qy. Ivo) de Eston p Thomas fitz Ralf, for her dower in the vills of Normanton and Eston, held by her former husband, John de Eston, but Mathew said it was his mother's inheritance (who was one of eight co-heirs), and his father could not endow his second wife out of it.

As to Basselaw, this, again, was one of the king's manors, and we learn nothing from Domesday, and it is the same with Froggat, which was part of this manor, and also with respect to Bubbeshill. Cardeburc is not traceable at present.

With regard to grants out of these properties, we find that Wm. de Avenel, Lord of Haddon, gave One Ash to Roche Abbey; this again, if Lysons has rightly identified it, was in the king's hands at Domesday, but possibly this was Ash in Sutton-on-the-Hill. We also find that he gave Conkesbury to the Abbot of Leicester, and here we find a true Ferrars connection, for this place is in Youlgrave, one of Henry de Ferrars' Domesday manors.

But perhaps the clearest evidence is to be extracted (almost dragged) from the history of Sutton-on-the-Hill. This was held by Henry de Ferrars at Domesday, and it contained Ash, Osleston, and Thurveston.

Ralf de Boscheville (probably the Ralf of the Red Book)

gave the church of Sutton to Tutbury, and John gave half the tithes of Osleston and Nether Thurvaston to Tutbury. He was probably the father of Odo, who held one of Wm. de Boscheville's knight's fees *tempe* Henry II.

Reginald Bassett attested a Rufford charter of Gerard de Furnival c. John.

English records failing to supply evidence, we must turn to Norman, and here we quickly discover a close connection between the Ferrars family in England and that of Avenel in Normandy. Perhaps the Avenels ranked even higher than the families of the Barons Fossiers, for just as in England the Ferrars granted manors to the Avenels, in Normandy the Avenels were lords of the Ferrars.

The author must refer the learned reader for an account of the Avénels to his history of the House of Arundel. In that work he has endeavoured to identify them with the great family of Picot de Say, and a direct connection between the Avenels and the Ferrars family is established by the marriage of Roger Albini, the King's Pincerna, and Wm. de Say, with two of the sisters of Hugh de Grent Mesnil, this Roger d'Ivri being brother of Nigel Albini, who married the sister of Wacheline de Ferrars. The chief seat of this family was at the Bois Avenel, in Landelles, near Biarz, in La Manche.

The Says or Avenels were knights of Roger Montgomery, and by him settled in Shropshire and various places in England about the time of the Conquest. The Chronique de Normandy names amongst the companions of the Conqueror, the Sire de Biars, and "Avenel de Biars."

The Chartulary of Marmontier (Bibl. Natl. de France) gives a grant, dated 1037, of the Church of St. Martin's de Belisme, by Hughes, son of John de Roceto, which was attested by Henry de Biars, his kinsman, who was ultimately his heir in 1067.

Sigembert de Biars and Ormenellus, surnamed Avenellus, gave a third of his rights in the same church to the same Abbey (Gal Christ. XI., part 153). (It will be remembered that the first Avenel of Haddon who attests Lenton Chartulary, 2 Henry I., only signs with a surname, a practice only in vogue at that period amongst very high personages.)

William Avenel, of Biars, 1082, gave the Church of Vezens

and the Priory of Biarz to the Abbey of La Couture, in the Diocese of Mans, Ralf, his brother, and Rainold (Ralf), his son, confirming the gift. This William Avenel had sons named William, Richard, Robert, and Hugh.

The Chartulary of Lessay, at St. Lo, records a grant of Richard Avenel, brother of William, confirmed 1126 by Henry I. Ralf and William Avenel both attested the charter of Wm. de Campo Ernulphi to the Abbey of Marmoutier, about 1088.

The Chartulary of Savigni (fol. 80, Cartulaire de Normandy— Rouen Libl.) proves distinctly that Wm. de Ferrars was a knight of Robert de Avenel's in Normandy, for he gave the land of Broilli D'oet with his consent to that foundation. The date of this charter is c. Henry II. Robert Earl Ferrars had made a grant of land in Northamptonshire to the same Abbey just previously.

Oliver fil Alain and Mary his wife, gave half the mill of Pasbray to the same foundation, with the consent of Ranulf de Avenel.

c. 1158. Wm. Avenel Siegneur de Biarrs mentions his three sons, Roland, Nicolas, and Oliver. Roland married Havis de Parigni. Oliver, who died in 1228, married Petronille de la Cheze, leaving Oliver his son.

The Chartulary of Mont St. Michael contains many entries relating to the family. About 1080, Ranulf Avenel and Hervey Avenel attested the charter of Robert Earl of Mortain, and he gave the Church of Sartilly to that foundation, which Ranulf, his son, confirmed about 1105. In 1121, William Avenel was senescal of the earl. That this is the same family appears most probable, from a grant of Ranulf Avenel of certain services in the vill of Coutance, the Honour of the St. Sauveur (Albini family), about 1100.

Ralf Avenel was a witness to a charter granted to the Priory of Mortain, A.D. 1082.

But the most pertinent fact to this enquiry is that Emma de Vernon, daughter of Baldwin Brionis, Earl of Devon (also called Baldwin de Insula), married William Avenel. Matilde, the daughter of Ralf Avenel (her son), married successively Robert, natural son of King Henry I., and Robert of Averanches, whose daughter and heir married Rainald de Courtney, and so founded that family in the West of England. The great importance of this connection exists in the great probability that the Vernons of Haddon were of the family of the Earls of Devon, and not of that of the Vernons of Chester, upon whom the heralds have affiliated them.

Now let us turn to the evidence of the Cartulary of the Abbey of Monteburg (the public library of Paris).

First at fol. 8 we find Richard Avenel granting the mill of Otelin to that foundation; to a charter of William de Vernon, granting land in the territory of the Albinis at St. Sauveur (Neelhuma), William Avenel and Richard, his sons, were witnesses. This is very important, as it emphasises the idea of the origin of Richard de Vernon, who married the daughter of William de Avenel of Haddon, showing that this William de Vernon actually had a son Richard at this period.

At fol. 101 we find a charter of Roger de Magnaville, Lord of Goelso . . . . granting the land which Oliver Avenel (no doubt another son of William) held of him, Stephen fil Roger de Magnaville and Roger, his uncle, being witnesses. Geoffry fil Robert de Magnaville held a tenement in Baskerville (fol. 8).

Fol. 103. Roger de Magnaville gave the church of Bernville, which William Avenel, Richard and Oliver, his sons, attested with William Magnaville.

Fol. 104. William Avenel confirms the grant of the land of Boscherville, which was of the fee of Robert Magnaville, and which they gave to Margaret, his wife, and Goisford, his son, with the consent of Count Baldwin (de Redvers) and Stephen de Magnaville.

For further information respecting the family of Magnaville and their relations, the author must refer the reader to his introduction to Mr. Glanville Richards' History of the House of Glanville, where he has referred to this interesting family.

It must not be forgotten that the Magnavilles, or Mandevills, were closely connected with the Rye family, Geoffry de Mandeville having married Eudo de Rye's daughter. Eudo at one time was the lord of all the property of the Vernons, Redvers, and Magnavilles referred to in the Monteburg Cartulary, having for some reason, perhaps as sheriff only, obtained the inheritance of the family of St. Sauveur.

Hardly less pertinent, and perhaps more necessary to the history of this fee, is that of the origin of the Vernons of Haddon.

Obviously the Heralds are entirely at sea on this subject, and have made some shocking guesses in order to confirm the theory of the identity of the Vernons of Haddon with the great family of Vernon of the County of Stafford in the time of Domesday.

It appears from Omerod's History of Cheshire that prior to this date it had been supposed that Richard de Vernon, who married the co-heir of Avenel of Haddon, was the son of Sir William Vernon, chief justice of Chester, who was a younger son of the Baron of Shipbrook ; but Omerod, and following him, his learned editor, the late Mr. T. Helsby, threw cold water upon this suggestion, without, however, absolutely rejecting it ; and it still holds its shameless head in Burke's Peerage, the only difference being that Sir Bernard Burke has married the heiress of Avenel to the Baron of Shipbrook himself. Omerod adds that it seems more probable that he was a descendant of Walter Vernon of Harlaston ; and if ever there was such a personage, this would be no doubt greatly more likely, for the dates absolutely disprove a descent from the justice of Chester. The marriage with the heiress of Haddon took place probably early in the reign of Richard I. or late in that of Henry II. Sir Wm. Vernon was justice of Chester 15 Henry III., some 50 years later. The author of the pedigree published by Sir Bernard Burke was therefore right as to the date in converting Sir Wm. from father to son of Sir Richard, but absolutely without authority for doing so, and more than this, in the direct face of authority, for these two knights, Richard of Shipbrook, and Richard of Haddon were separate, though contemporary personages.

Burke's Peerage again states that Richard Vernon obtained a grant of Peak Castle in 1252. This does not appear upon the Pipe Rolls, but the name does ; and it seems that Richard de Vernon was in that year an attorney or pledge for one Robt. de Warth, a very different affair.

Shaw, in his History of Staffordshire, has taken to task Collins and Edmonson, who are the authors of the absurd Histories of the Vernon Pedigree, very severely, and he has exposed the fact that these untrustworthy writers have actually only given three descents from William Vernon of Domesday to Sir William the justice of Chester, a period of 300 years ; and in

the short space of 99 years has given 10 descents from him to
Sir Richard of the time of Henry VI.; and in writing his own
account, showing how history was then written, he adds, " I have
inserted a Sir Richard partly in conjecture; I rejected several
others." Mr. Helsby, in commenting upon this wonderful
pedigree, states that the writer of Shaw's account was a learned
antiquary named Samuel Pope Wolferston. It is fortunate that
he was so honest as to admit that he made up his pedigrees
partly by conjecture.

Now the groundwork of Mr. Wolferston's account is a charter
of Hugh, Earl of Chester, and of Matilde his countess, granting to Walter Vernon the land and honour of Harlaston, which
Walter, his grandfather, held of the Earl of Chester (not
naming him), and which was then part of the dower of Maud,
his countess. However this may be, it was in the king's hands
in 11 Henry II., for the sheriff then accounts for 4s. 6d. rent
for it. This charter is set out in Shaw, but apparently is a
forgery. In the first place, Harlaston was never an honour, but
only part of the king's manor, none of the witnesses can be
identified, except the third, Eustace fitz John, who died at a
very advanced age in 1157, before Hugh, the Earl, succeeded
(1158); and the third place is hardly that in which we should
expect to find so important a personage as Eustace fitz John.
The first witness is one Richard fil the Earl of Gloucester,
apparently a mythical personage.

Maud, the countess, was the daughter of Robert, the son of
King Henry I., who married Maud, the daughter of William
Avenel.

But the Vernons were disseized, according to this charter,
for the lady held it in dower; and we do not learn from the
charter itself of which Earl of Chester, Walter, the grandfather
of the donee, held it. Looking at the dates, this would carry
us back to Domesday; and then we find a Walter de Vernon,
and Wachiline a nephew of Walter de Vernon, as well as
Richard Vernon, holding lands of the Earl of Chester, but not
the manor of Harlaston, then part of Clifton, the king's manor;
and subsequently Robert Marmion held it of the Earl of
Ferrers. If we could only rely upon this charter, it would
perhaps give a complete pedigree for the family. As it is,
there is no evidence, as there should be, of any kind to support

it, and having regard to its intrinsic improbabilities, we can only regard it with suspicion.

We know nothing of any Walter Vernon, of Harlaston, in the time of Henry II., though we have evidence, from the Staffordshire Pipe Rolls of 6 Richard I., that Haslaston had, previously to that date, been the property of a Richard Vernon, and that he had some time previously forfeited it, for the sheriff accounted for 40s. rents, proof, General Wrottesley considers, that he was an outlaw. The Derbyshire Pipe Rolls for the same year, it must be remembered, show that Richard de Vernon and Simon de Basset were each farming half the land of Avenel, of Basselaw, then part of the Honour of Peverel. It also shows that Robert Avenel was then an outlaw; and the Bucks. and Bedfordshire Rolls still add to the puzzle, for they show that Simon Basset paid 100 marcs for having the land of Richard de Vernon, which he took with his wife, which was the inheritance of Simon's wife; one Richard Vernon, an outlaw at Harlaston, Stafford, another (or the same), farming his wife's inheritance, and a third (or again the same), wrongfully enjoying the land belonging to his wife's sister in Bucks. and Beds.

It should be noted, however, that General Wrottesley interprets the Bucks. entry as proof that Richard Vernon's inheritance had passed to a female. This, however, appears to the author to be erroneous, but if accurate, it itself disposes of the alleged Harlaston descent.

In 7 Richard I., Richard Vernon's Harlaston estate was still in the king's hands; but in 8 Richard I. he agreed to pay £20 for twenty librates of land in Staffordshire, which General Wrottesley, with much reason, assumes was Harlaston.

There is an entry in the Staffordshire Roll of Richard Vernon being fined in 22 Henry II.; this was possibly on the occasion of his forfeiture. Testa de Nevil shows that in 39 Henry III., Richard de Vernon held Harlaston of the Earl of Derby. Now, it is quite clear that the Earl of Derby inherited some of the Staffordshire estates of the Earl of Chester through his marriage with Agnes, daughter of Hugh, Earl of Chester, the alleged grantor of Harlaston to Walter Vernon; but it is not so clear that Harlaston was ever part of them. Clifton, no doubt, was held by the Earl. But this was a separate manor, and no account shows that the Chester family had ever held it. Gough's Camden II., p. 394, gives a record, 27 Henry III., rot. 11a, in proof, but this has not yet been found.

There was a family named de Herlaston in the time of King John, of whom nothing has been published. In 1 John, Robert de Herlaston was essoinator in a Clifton suit, and in 6 John William de Herlaston, and Amicia his wife, in a suit (which was settled) between themselves, and one Henry de Dernston, in which William fitz Herbert was called to warranty.

Huntback's pedigree of Vernon makes William de Vernon the son of Richard, who married the heiress of Avenel, die 26 Henry III., leaving two sons : Richard, who died s. p. 27 Henry III. ; and Robert, who died without male issue, leaving a daughter and heiress, who married Gilbert le Francis, and whose son assumed the name of Vernon. Other accounts assert that Sir William married the daughter and heir of Gilbert Francis of Harlaston, and no question can be raised as to the fact that Gilbert Francis was Lord of Harlaston *tempe* Henry III. and Edward I., and that he died seized of it, though we have not any inquisition which proves by what title he acquired it. But the inquisition taken at his death in 6 Edward I. shows that he held Haddon, Roulesley, Basselaw, and Bobenhall of the Earl of Derby, and that Richard was his son and heir, aged fifteen. The inquisition after his death, taken at Westmorland, shows that Richard, his son, was then married to the daughter of Matthew de Harcla, and this after Gilbert's decease.

Richard fil Gilbert Francis must have died young, and we have no inquisition at his death. His son Richard died 16 Edward II. (forty-four years after Gilbert le Francis' death); and he then held Harlaston and Appleby, Parva of the Honour of Tutbury (then in the king's hands), which Richard, his father, held in 8 Edward II., as also the Derbyshire estates.

Now these dates prove conclusively that Sir William Vernon did not obtain these manors from Francis, for he held them at his death, years after the decease of the former, and yet it is clear that they were in the hands of a Richard Vernon in 27 Henry III., from whom Gilbert le Francis can only have obtained them by marrying his daughter, or by purchase, for in truth there is no evidence of the existence of any daughter of this Richard, the suggestion being a mere guess.

This is brought down to a still closer date by a record of Trinity Term, 42 Henry III., given by General Wrottesley, from which it appears that Robert Vernon was alive that year, for he and William de Camville were sued by Robert de Beverley ; and it would seem that Richard de Vernon was still alive, for Walter de Palton sued for land in Swinfen, which a Richard de Vernon lost by a default. He however may have been of the Cheshire family.

On 26th June, 1272, Margery, widow of Peter Anesy, and Matthew de Anesy, sued Richard de Vernon, with Gilbert le Francis and another, which seems to show that Richard Vernon survived longer than is supposed, and that Gilbert Francis, his successor, was associated with him in the inheritance.

Another very useful series of dates concerning the Tymmore property shows the succession still more clearly, the mill of which place was held by the Vernons under the Sage family.

Here, again, the Heralds, in their anxiety to magnify the antiquity of the family, have endeavoured to show that the Vernons held Tymmore as early as the reign of Henry I., and they produce a lease as of that date from Petronilla le Sage to William le Vernon ; but William, son of this Petronilla, was living 25 Henry III., when he gave a fresh lease of the mill for 20 years.

Richard Vernon obtained a renewal of the lease in 41 Henry III. for 19 years ; and Gilbert le Francis obtained a lease in 4 Edward I., which Richard Vernon, son of Gilbert le Francis, assigned in 8 Edward II. to Richard, his son. As we have seen from the Inquisition Post Mortem, he was living this year.

Appleby Parva came into the family of Vernon through the marriage, *tempe* John, of Wm. de Vernon, said to be the Justice of Chester, with the heiress of Stockport ; in the same way Marple came into the family. This was granted by Ralf, Earl of Chester, to Robert fil Robert de Stockport ; whose grant was attested by Philip de Orreby, Justice of Chester, 1210-29, and Wm. de Vernon. There is a suit in 21 Edward I. by Geoffry de Camville against Richard Vernon for two acres of land in

Camville ; but Richard was then in prison, and the suit was respited.

Of the family of Francis little is known. They came into the Vernon property between the years 1272 when Richard Vernon was alive, and 1276-7, when Gilbert obtained a renewal of the lease of Tymmore ; how is yet not positively known.

But this is known ; Gilbert le Francis, at his death, held a great number of small properties in Cumberland and Westmoreland, not of inheritance, but which he farmed. He, however, held one property there which had been held by a John le Francis, whose heir he evidently was. If it could be shown that he was the son of this man, we might get the pedigree still a generation higher, for a John, son of Robert le Francis was well known in Staffordshire. In 11 Henry III. there was an Assize in Stafford, if Robert, father of John, held the manor of Huse, which Robert Howell then occupied, which was settled by giving up one-fifth of the manor to John.

The Staffordshire Pipe Rolls show that Robert le Francis was repeatedly fined for selling wine contrary to the assize. This occurred in 1189, and in several years afterwards. In 5 Richard I. Robt. le Francis was fined 40s. for making a false claim. In 1 John he was again fined for selling wine in the house of Tatmanslow. 11 John he was found guilty of intruding into the land of Wm. de Pailes, in Handsworth, whilst he was in prison. He was a native of Newcastle.

The result of the whole facts seems to indicate that the first property obtained by the Vernons of Haddon was Haddon itself, that Haslington was the next, which was obtained by the payment of £20 to the king in 6 Richard I., that the payment was accepted probably because it had been Vernon property, but which was forfeited as early as 11 Henry II., and was still in the king's hands ; that possibly it had belonged to the ancestors of this Richard Vernon, or merely to some of the name ; and that he was brought into England through his marriage with the heiress of Avenel, he probably being one of the family connected with the Avenels in Normandy, and a Vernon of the house of Briones or Redvers.

In giving this account of the Avenel family, the author desires to acknowledge the great obligation he is under to that eminent antiquary Sir John Maclean, who, subsequently to the publication of the History of the House of Arundel, furnished the author with very valuable references to the history of this family. It is not always possible to acknowledge one's obligations to others, though, in a case where much information is given, it is a positive duty to do so. The author was unpleasantly reminded of this very recently by reading in the Archæological Journal for Yorkshire an account of a family, the majority of the notices concerning which were given by him to the writer of it, who has not thought it fair to make any kind of acknowledgment, though privately he was grateful and very anxious to obtain further information.

18.—*Galf de Firetry held one fee, which Maurice his son gave to the White Monastery, who then held it.*

19.—*Hubert de Curtenei held three fees, of which Stephen, his nephew, then held two, and the Templars the third.*
NOTE.—This name appears to be written Curcun in the Black Book. Owing to the similarity of the letters t and c, many records relating to the Curcun, or Curzon family, are transcribed wrongly, Curton.

20.—*Will. fil Oton held one fee, which the White Monks of Tame then held.*
NOTE.—A William fil Oto married Maud, daughter of William de Dive, by Matilda, daughter of Geoffry de Waterville and Ascelina Peverel. This Geoffry was a descendant of Azelin, the tenant of Geoffry Ascelin of Domesday.

21.—*Pagan de Niveton held half a fee, and gave it to the White Monks of Combremere.*
NOTE.—The Pipe Rolls of 18 and 25 Henry II. mention a Godwin de Newton, and 34 Henry II. mentions an Artur.

22.—*Robt. de Chauces held one fee.*
NOTE.—Goisfred Ascelin held Turalveston at Domesday, and Robt. de Calz succeeded to part of his inheritance. See more of this baron hereafter under the certificate of Geoffry de Anselin.

23.—*Henry de Cuneigeston held one fee, which William de Hastings then held.*

24.—*John Turbelvill held one fee, which Henry Hosato then held.*

NOTE.—We know little of the first family in Derbyshire ; but Henry Hosato was a well-known personage, who resided at Averham or Egrum, Notts., which he acquired by marriage with Avice, the daughter of Adam Tison and sister of Wm. of the great baronial family, knights of the Mowbrays.

25.—*William de Trusley, and then Robert, his son, held one knight's fee.*

26.—*Atrop Hastings held one fee.*

THESE KNIGHTS WERE ENFEOFFED BY MY GRANDFATHER, WHICH I NOMINATE.

[There is an erasure here in the original, as if the word had been originally (proavus) great-grandfather, for which no doubt it was intended, the next class of knights having been enfeoffed out of the demesne of his son, the maker's grandfather.]

27.—*Nicolas de Breylesford, and then Henry, his son, who held one fee.*

NOTE.—Testa de Nevil shows that Henry de Brailsford then held one fee in Breylesford.

The Book of Aids states that Henry de Brailsford then held half a fee in Brailsford and half in Wingerworth, formerly the fee of Ralf, his father. This is one of the finest Derbyshire pedigrees ; they were probably of English origin, descendants of Elfine, who at the time of Domesday held Brailsford, Osmaston, Balden, and Thurvaston. Ailson de Brailsford, probably the same person, gave Osmaston to Tutbury, which created a great feud between Odinel de Ford and the Prior some time afterwards. It is to be hoped that this pedigree may be clearly established.

28.—*William fitz Herbert held one fee.*

NOTE.—Testa de Nevil shows that Wm. fitz Herbert held three parts of a fee in Ash.

1175, John fitz Herbert was surety for his lord.

William fitz Herbert attested the charter of exchange between Dun and Pantoul.

29.—*Wm. de St. Quinten held half a fee.*

NOTE.—This family in the time of King John were represented by Robert de St. Quinten, who married Albreda, the daughter of Jordan Chevercourt.

30.—*David de Stanton held half a fee.*

NOTE.—Adam de Stanton, and William, his brother, attested the earl's charter to William Pantoul.

Testa de Nevil shows that Robert fil William ˙Stanton held half a knight's fee in Stony Stanton. Several families of this name were scattered about the county. One family was identical with the Pincernas of Belvoir; whilst another, settled at Kelum, were as clearly of the house of Albini of that Honour. They were probably identical with the family of Abney.

31.—*Ernald de Bec held half a fee.*

NOTE.—Testa de Nevil shows that Robert de Tuke and Galf de Bec held ⅓ of one fee in Milton.

G. de Bak and J. de Bak are mentioned in the charter of Wm., Earl Ferrars. Possibly they were of the Bakepuz family.

And Arnald and Henry de Bec were sureties for the earl in 23 Henry II.

Henry de Bec and Avice, his wife, answered to a plea of the forest in 32 Henry II.

This name is frequently mentioned in Derbyshire records down to the time of King Henry V.

32.—*Adam fil Swanne held one fee, then held by his heirs.*

NOTE.—This is probably a descendant of Swain of Colley, *tempe* Domesday; he is probably identical with Swain fil ·Swain, a Thane, of the same period, who then held Chisworth direct of the king. His name would indicate that he was of Danish origin, and he would therefore readily be accepted tenant by a Norman lord.

Swain Cilt (the younger) was probably the same person. He held 10 manors under King Edward which Walter de Aincourt held at Domesday.

Adam fil Swain is mentioned in a Pipe Roll of 12 Henry II., and traces of the family are to be found at a late date. In all probability the family of de Colley, who continued resident at Cowley, were of the same family. This, though not now an important family, is a very interesting one.

33.—*Walter del Bec held one fee, which William de Cheisnei then held.*

34.—*Hugo fil Richard held one fee.*

NOTE.—Robert fil Richard de Normanton was one of the knights of the Earl de Ferrars.

35.—*Roger le Grendon held one fee.*

NOTE.—The Testa de Nevil shows that William de Grendon held half a fee of Bubbersville of the old feoffment of Robt. St. George.

It is probable that the fee was at Bradley, which, according to the chronicle of Thos. de Musca, was held by Serlo de Grendon, who married the sister of William fil Ralf, the Justiciary of Normandy, Sheriff of Nottingham and Derby, *tempe* Henry II.

Serlo de Grendon was living 24-33 Henry II.

27 Henry II. Walkelin de Bradly is mentioned ; William, John Henry, and Robert de Grendon at a later date ; Hugo fil Ralf in Kirby's Quest, Thomas, *tempe* Henry VI.

36.—*Robert de Albini held one fee.*

NOTE.—This family has already been mentioned under Tenant No. 3.. It is not clear whether this Robert was the son of William of the time of Henry II., or his uncle, as the first Robert died without male issue, the latter relationship is the most probable. Here, doubtless, we get the stem of the family of Abney in Hope (which Derbyshire historians have mistaken for Habenai, the wasted manor of Wm. Peverel), who are now represented by the Abneys of Willersley. The proofs of this pedigree, which are very voluminous, for it is one of the greatest in the county, must be deferred to the Parochial History.

37.—*Ralf fitz William half a fee which Hunfry de Tolka of Steple then held, and half a one which Maurice held.*

NOTE.—Testa de Nevil shows that Robert de Tuke held one-third of a fee with Galf de Bec in Hilton.

1178. Hericus de Tuche was one of the sureties of the earl.

38.—*Landries, which then Jordan, his son, held one fee.*

THESE (LAST 13) KNIGHTS' FEES THE BARON, MY GRANDFATHER, GRANTED OUT OF HIS OWN DEMESNE.

[The Red Book omits the word grandfather, but it is supplied by the Black Book.]

THESE THE EARL MY FATHER ENFEOFFED OF HIS OWN DEMESNE.

39.—*Hunfred de Tolka held one fee.* (See No. 37.)

40.—*Galf de Briencourt held one fee.*

41.—*Galf Salvage held half a fee.*

NOTE.—At the same time, or a little later, Robert fil Galfry (Savage) held Hints and Tipton of Robert de Stafford. At Domesday these manors were held by the Bishop. In 1156 Robert fil Galfry and Helius, his brother, attested a charter of Walter, the Bishop.

The Testa de Nevil shows that Galf le Salvage still held one fee in Hints, and Galfry fil Warin held one in Tibeton (Tipton), which he had obtained in marriage with the daughter of Galf le Salvage.

Kirkby's Quest shows that Hugh de Meynil held half a fee in Hints and Tibeton, having married Philippa, sister and co-heir of Galf Savage, who died without issue, 32 Henry II.

Helius fil Galfry le Savage held Pershaw (Worcestershire).

Galf le Savage granted land to Polesworth Priory, so did William and Robert his brothers (Warwickshire).

4 Henry II. Galf le Salvage paid 10 marcs for a venison trespass (Derbyshire).

7 Richard I. Galf Salvage paid 100 m. for having his father's lands in Warwickshire.

It would be interesting to learn whether Robert le Sauvage, who obtained a grant of the marriage of Havise fil Wm. fil Walkelin with Steynsby in 3 John, was of this family. Very possibly he was identical with Robert, mentioned in the Polesworth Cartulary. Inasmuch as William fil Walkelin was a Ferrars, it is highly probable that a knight of that house should secure his inheritance.

42.—*Robert de Pir held half a fee.*

NOTE.—His fee would seem to be in Hilton.

This knight, though holding so small a fee, was a person of great consequence. He seems to have been sheriff of the county in the first year of Henry II., and in the sixth, when Robert Earl of Ferrers died, he appears to have answered for his estate, probably as farmer or as senescal.

1178. Wm. de Piri was surety for the earl.

Thomas de Piru gave 3 bovates of land in Hilton to the Church of Marston (Tutbury Cartulary). He was one of the witnesses to the earl's charter to Maurice de Luvitot.

43.—*William Giffard held half a fee.*

44.—*Maurice de Turtey held half a fee.*

45.—*Adam Vicompte Baroches held half a fee.*

46—*Wm. de Tolka held a quarter of a fee.* ((See Tenant No. 37.)

47.—*Hugo de Gobion held one-third of one fee.*

48.—*Somerville, Walter de, held ¼ of one fee.*

NOTE.—The Black Book notes that Adam, Sheriff of Berkshire, and William de Tolka, held this part fee.

Robert, Earl of Ferrars, gave four bovates of land, which he obtained in exchange with Walter de Somerville, to Burton Abbey. Walter de Somerville held Wichnore and Terescob, in Staffordshire, of Robert de Stafford, and which Roger de Somerville held at the time of Testa de Nevil.

49.—*William de Ferrars held one manor of the lord, his (the Black Book states my) father, for which he made the service of four knights.*

This was possibly William fitz Wachel, Lord of Steynesby.

THESE NINE AND ONE-THIRD PARTS OF ONE KNIGHT'S FEE MY FATHER GAVE OUT OF HIS OWN DOMINION.

Baggarugge is mine. For sixty knights should I do service to you and Memstrums (Memtenin in the Black Book), Main holds against me. So much may it please you.

Of Cruc I am disseized without judgment, which is one fee.

THIS IS THE SUM OF THE OLD AND NEW KNIGHTS—LXXIX. KNIGHTS, AND A THIRD PART OF ONE FEE.

LIST OF TENANTS OF THE GREAT BARONY OF
WILLIAM, EARL OF FERRARS, FROM THE
YEARS 1066–1088 TO 1162 (PROBABLE DATE OF
CERTIFICATE).

[The number preceding the name is that of the tenancy;
the number at the end, of the page where the account of such
tenancy is to be found.]

45-8. Adam, Sheriff of Berkshire, 310.
3. Albini, William fil Nigel, 281.
3. Albini, Robert, 308.
36.   „   „
6. Bakepuz, Robert, 285.
7. Baskerville, Henry, 286.
31. Bec, Ernald; John his son, 307.
33. Bec, Walter, 308.
45-8. Berkshire, Sheriff of, 310.
16. Boscheville, William; Ralf his son, 293.
27. Breilsford, Nic.; Henry his son, 306.
40. Briencourt, Galf, 309.
12. Cambries, Henry, 290.
14. Camera, Galf, 291.
22. Chaucis, Robert, 305
19. Curtenei, Hubert; Stephen his nephew, 305
23. Cuneigeston, Henry, 305.
4. Curzon, Rich.; Robert his son, 282.
9. Dun, Robert; James his son, 287.
49. Ferrars, William, 310.

16. Fifehead, Rich, 292.
18. Firetry, Galf (qy. Tirecer), 305.
43. Giffard, Will, 310.
14. Goldington, Peter, 291.
47. Gobion, Hugo, 310.
35. Grendon, Roger, 308.
10. Gresley, Reginald, 288.
15. Harcourt, Yvo (see Heriz), 291.
26. Hastings, Aitrop, 306.
23.   „   William, 305.
28. Herbert fitz William, 306.
24. Hosato, Henry, 305.
17. John, Odo fitz, 293.
38. Landries; Jordan his son, 308.
4. Luvitot, Robert, 289.
16. Marmion, Galf, Heirs of, 291.
5. Montgomery, Walter, 283.
21. Niveton, Pagan, 305.
20. Oton, William fil, 305.
11. Pantoul, William, 289.
10. Parvus, Ralf, 288.
42. Pir, Robert, 309.
14. Ralf, Robert fil, 291.
34. Richard, Hugo fil, 308.

41. Salvage, Galf, 309.

1 & 2. Sewell, Henry fil ; Fulc
his brother, 279.

29. St. Quinten, William,
306.

13. Seyle, William ; Ralf
his son, 290.

48. Somerville, Walter, 310.

30. Stanton, David, 307.

32. Swain, Adam fil, 307.

44. Turtey, Maurice, 310.

39. Tolka, Hump, 308.

46-8.   „   William, 310.

25. Trusley, William ;
Robert his son, 306.

24. Turbelville, John, 305.

37. William, Ralf fil, 308.

8. Walkelin, Robert ;
Robert his son, 286.

15   „   William, 291.

CHAPTER V.

No. 2.—The Charter of Ralf Hanselin (Anselin.)

TO HIS LORD HENRY, KING OF ENGLAND, RAD ANSEL, HEALTH AND FAITHFUL SERVICE: KNOW YE THAT IN THE TIME OF KING HENRY YOUR GRANDFATHER I HAD THE FOLLOWING KNIGHTS OF THE OLD FEOFF-MENT

1.—*Will. Ansel. de Walesby* (*in one copy Wagerby*) *held two knights' fees.*

NOTE.—Part of this manor with Kirkton or Schedrington, and Wilgebi was soke to Grimston, some of it soke to Roger de Busli's Manor of Tuxforde, some to Goisfred de Hanselin's soc of Laxington. Wm. Lanceline's manors seem to have been in all these parishes. Wm. Lanceline (Ansel) gave to Wm. fitz Eudo de Hibaldeston with Cecilia his daughter in frank marriage 1 bovat in Walesby. Alan fil Wm. Lancelin, of Kirkton, gave his woods there to Robert de Laxington. 6 Edward II. Robt., son of Robert Lanceline, still held land in Kirkton.

Rad de Wadeland in Walesby gave to Rufford Abbey the services of John de la Chause, of Walesby, Wm. his brother, Wm. fil Henry, Nic his brother, Robt. D'aubeni, and Rich fil Philip for their services in Walesby.

1 Henry VIII. Wm. Bradbourne held land in Walesby, Wellawe, and Kirton.

22

A William Hanselin attested a charter of Ralf Silvans to Rufford Abbey concerning land at Wilibi of the fee of Gilbert de Gant, who died 1156. (Mr. Saville's charters at Rufford Abbey.)

2.—Walter de Derington held one knight's fee.

3.—Rad de Middleton held one knight's fee.

4.—Walter de Digby and William between them held two parts of 1 fee.
NOTE.—This manor was probably in North Leverton.
2 Edward III. Robt. de Dyggeby and Sibell his wife fined with Adam de Everingham, of Laxton, concerning this manor.

5, 6, 7.—Richard de Martinwast and William Sirewast and Puellus de Belcapo held three fees.
NOTE.—In the time of King Henry I. Robert Martinwast, with the assent of Richard de Haia his lord and of Hugo his brother, granted land in the marsh of Benedicts Ville to Monteburg.

8.—Ralf fil Geremond held two fees. (See Robert de Chauz, Charter No. 8.)
NOTE.—This knight, no doubt, was the father of Wm. fitz Ralf, Justiciar of Normandy and Sheriff of Nottinghamshire and Derbyshire, whose history is unknown at present. Eyton, indeed, doubts whether he was sprang from English parents, but there seems to be no ground for this opinion. Thomas de Muscam relates that he was lord of half Ockbrook and of Alvaston *cu soca.* Ockbrook was clearly one of Geoffrey Ascelin's manors, and it seems to have passed to the Bardolfs as heirs of Ralf Hanselin. This must, therefore, have been one of his fees, and as Alvaston was also a fee of Geoffrey Ascelin's, it was, no doubt, the other.

9.—Robert fil Thomas held half a fee.
NOTE.—This fee was probably in Cuckney, where Roger de Busli had a manor which Goisfred his man held. This Thomas of Cuckney was the grandson of Joceus le Fleming, who came into England at the Conquest, and son of Richard his son, who married a cousin of the Earl Ferrars. Thomas, his son, founded Welbec.

10.—*Robert de Bernecot and Robt. fil Galfry held half a fee.*
(See note to No. 15.)

12.—*Henry and Roger de Westburg held two parts of one-fifth of one fee.*

NOTE.—Westburg is a manor in Lincolnshire which became the property of Robert de Cauz, the successor to part of the manors of Geoffrey Hansclin. Adam de Everingham settled this manor on Thomas de Southwell in 4 Edward II., probably as trustee for himself.

13.—*Roger Bussard held one-twelfth of one fee of the purchase of the Bishop Robert Bloet, whose mother he married, which I hold of you in chief of that land, the Bishop disseized me this same land. Ralf fil Hugh Crumwell holds.*

NOTE.—This is a well-known family settled in Lincolnshire and Leicestershire at the time of Domesday, tenants of Robert Todeni, lord of Belvoir, and, indeed, the progenitors of the House of Albini, one member of which succeeded to the inheritance of Belvoir by marriage with a co-heir of Robert Todeni. They acquired the name of Bosco Rohardi (here abbreviated) from their residence at the place, part of the Honour of St. Sauveur in the Cotentin, the hereditary possession of the family. (See the author's history of the House of Arundel.)

In the Anniversaria of Belvoir Priory is to be found the name of Helias Borrohard. He is probably identical with Helias de Albini, whose charter, attested by Audierno, his brother, is to be found in f. 120-b of that MS. (Harl MSS. 2044.)

Wm. fil Hugh disseized 100 solidates of land which I gave to my son of my own demesne.

THESE ARE ALL THE OLD FEOFFMENTS MADE IN THE TIME OF HENRY YOUR FATHER.
THESE ARE THE NEW.

14.—*Alexr. de Cressi held half a fee.*
NOTE.—Roger de Cressi died 3 John. Cecilia, his widow, the daughter of Gervase de Clifton claims dower against his son William.

Wm. Cressi, of Markham (seal, three crescents and a bend), settled the manor of Saxelby and advowson of Brodholm on her. Roger de Cressi married Isabella, sister and heir of Wm. fil Wm. fil Roscilin (de Rya), who granted a mill in Hunting-field to Sibton Priory. (Harl MS. 2044).

15.—*Rad fil Galfry held half a fee.*

NOTE.—This fee was probably in Kirkton, or perhaps in Eycring. Robert fil Galfry de Kirkton, held a toft there, and granted it to Robt. fil Nicolas the Baker of Tuxford which Richard fil Toke held of Galfry his father, who gave it to Albreda his wife and Robt. his son. Robt. the Baker afterwards gave it to Rufford Abbey. (See Rufford Cartulary.)

16.—*German fil Simon held half a fee.*

17.— *Wm. Burdet held half a fee.*

NOTE.—This fee was probably in Kirkton.

Burdet of Bramcote, Warwick, obtained Foremark, Derby-shire, through the marriage with the heiress of Francis.

Alice de Bosco, heir of John Burdon, gave a wood in Kirkton to Robt. de Laxington, which Gumbert held.

John fil Sir John Burden, Kt. 6 Edward 2.

25 Edward III. Sir John Burden of Mapelbec and Elizabeth his wife conveyed them over to John de Ascam and another.

18.—*Wm. de Linc held half a fee.*

19.—*Galf fil Roger held half a fee.*

NOTE.—It is not quite clear whether these last four knights did not jointly hold the same half fee.

20.—*Ralf fil Roger de Bileston held half a fee.*

NOTE.—Hugh fitz Roger was on the jury concerning the Forest rights with Ralf Hanselin early in Henry II.'s reign. He was seneschal of Philip de Strelley, 4 Henry III.

7 John. Philip de Strelly fined to have the posthumous daughter of Richard fitz Roger to wife.

21.—*Galf fil Gilbert held half a fee.*

22.—*Reginald de Radclive held half a fee.*

Anselinus de Radclive attested Robert fitz Ralf's charter of land at Sutton Passeis to Lenton, given for the repose of the soul of Adelina his wife.

23.—*John de Galdeges held half a fee.*

24.—*Galfry de Fulbec held half a fee.*

NOTE.—Little is known of the connection of this knight with this county, or, indeed, of his family; but by the aid of the Rotuli Curiæ Regis and other Rolls, a fair pedigree may be constructed. They were knights of the Earls Conan and Alan of Brittany, and hereditary constables of Richmond Castle, though, as their surname of de Bosco confirms, they were probably of the family of Magnaville, or Stuteville. (See the author's Introduction to the House of Glanville.) They were closely connected with the Albinis of Belvoir, and attested many of their charters. Roald, son of this Galfry, and his father, for they were of the same name, was constable of Newark, and Alan de Bosco, son of Roald, was a frequent witness to the charters of Leonia, the widow of Robert de Stuteville, the heiress of half the barony of Hubert fitz Ralf.

Alan fil Galf, probably the same person as Alan fil Roald, held land in Pickering in 1 Richard I. As his ancestor had done previously, so did Wm. and Walter de Bosco, his successors. There is reason to believe that the latter is identical with Walter de Bosco, of Barlbro', *temp.* Henry III., who was undoubtedly the progenitor of the family of Sitwell, of Eckington, now represented by Sir George Sitwell, Bt., M.P. Although the connecting link has not yet been discovered, many facts have been adduced which render it most probable, an Assize Roll of the time of Edward I., establishing the fact beyond all doubt that the father of Simon Sitwell of that date was the son of this Walter de Bosco of Barlbro'. The names Sitwell and Stutevill are probably identical. In the Testa de Nevil the Lord of Eckington is styled "Sotville."

25.—*Ulfus de Seccobiton held half a fee.*

NOTE.—This is a very interesting and purely English family. This knight is, in all probability, the progenitor of the well-known Derbyshire family of de Hathersage.

The place here indicated, Seccobiton, is no doubt Skegbi, which formed part of Marnham, a portion of Roger de Busli's great lordship. Ulf held Marnham in the time of the Confessor, and probably there and in Sceggbi he still continued to hold under Roger de Busli, who supplanted him. He is probably identical with Ulf Fenesc, who with the Archbishop of York and the Countess Godiva, had espécial privilege with regard to soc and sac, showing that he was one of the chief thanes of the county. He or his son, perhaps both, were tenants of Walter de Gant, in Eicring. Wulf fil Ulf de Eicring gave three acres there of that earl's demesne to the monks of Rufford to keep Godwin, his son, till he should be of age in their house.

A Walter de Skeggbi is also to be found mentioned in the Rufford Chartulary.

Ulfus, or Wulfus fil Ulf had also two sons, named Gilbert and William, to whom, with the consent of Maud St. Liz, his wife, William Albini, lord of Belvoir, gave ten acres of land in Eicring. Gilbert de Sceggbi, a grandson of Wulfus, also gave land, part of this grant, to Rufford.

Mathew, son of William, son of Wulfus, was fined for some forest trespass in that remarkable Assize (given at page 119) of the 22 Henry II. He was the first Mathew de Hathersage. He probably settled in North Derbyshire, owing to the connection of his father with the Albinis, or Abneys of Hope, also surnamed de Stoke, a branch of the Albini family of Belvoir. The Chartulary now at Rufford Abbey gives evidence of great interest on this point, which will be duly detailed in the Parochial History.

The history of this family is a remarkably clear instance of the stability of the English race under Norman dominance, though in all probability it was by no means uncommon. The notable circumstance here is the retention of their ancient name to so late a date, the result, probably, of their high rank prior to the Norman Conquest.

26.—*Wm. de Westburg.* (See note to No. 12.)

27.—*Adam de Cressi.* (See note to No. 14)

AND WITH THE OTHERS IN MY OWN DEMESNE I MAKE TWENTY-FIVE KNIGHTS, WHOSE SERVICES I OWE TO YOU.

TENANTS OF RALF HANSELIN, *TEMPE* HENRY II.

1. Ansel, William.
7. Bellocampo, Puellus.
10. Bernecot, Robert
20. Bileston, Ralf fil Roger.
13. Bussard, Rog.
17. Burdet, William.
14. Cressi, Alex.
27.   „   Adam.
2. Derington, Walter.
4. Digby, Walter.
   „   William
24. Fulbec Galf.
23. Galdeges, John.
15.   „   Ralf.
10. Galfry, Robert.

8. Geremund, Ralf fitz.
21. Gilbert, Galfry fil.
18. Lincoln, William.
5. Martinwast, Rd.
3. Middleton, Rad.
22. Radclive, Reginald.
19. Roger, Galf fil.
20.   „   Ralf.
16. Simon, German fil.
6. Sirewast, William.
9 Thomas, Robert fil.
23. Ulfus de Scobbiton.
12. Westburg, Henry.
   „   Roger.
26.   „   William.

CHAPTER VI.

No. 3.—Carta Roger de Buron.

TO HENRY, THE KING OF ENGLAND, DUKE OF
NORMANDY, AQUITAINE, AND EARL OF
ANJOU. ROGER DE BURON.—HEALTH.—CON-
CERNING MY KNIGHTS WHO HELD LAND IN
THE TIME OF KING HENRY I. KNOW THAT
THEY ARE:

1.—*William de Heriz who holds two fees.*

2.—*Roger de Cotingstock holds in Cortinstock and Rempston
two fees.*
NOTE.—This Roger de Cortingstock confirmed the grant of
Andrew de Cortingstock and of Robert, his son (Roger's
father), to Lenton.
Robert fil Andrew de Cortingstock was a knight of Hugh de
Buron's in 1147. John de Cortingstock was a witness to a
Sutton Passeis charter in 1278.

3.—*Patricius de Rosel holds one knight's fee.*

4.—*Albertus, who my father enfeoffed after the death of King
Henry, holds one knight's fee, and I myself do service for four
knights' fees of my demesne.*

CHAPTER VII.

No. 4.—Carta Ihascuil Musard.

OF THE OLD FEOFFMENT.

1.—*Aitorp Hastings, five fees.* (See No. 7 of the Earl de Ferrars' knights.)

2.—*Oliver de Mara, two fees.*

3.—*Maen de Hatrop, two fees.*

4.—*Walter de Eston, two fees.*

5.—*Galfrey de Cheleworth, one fee.*

The sum of his old feoffment, twelve knights, and of his own demesne of the new feoffment. Two and a half, and one-fifth of one fee namely,

6.—*William de Caisneto, half a fee.*

7.—*The widow of Richard Musard holds in dower two fees.*

8.—*Fulco de Musters, one-fifth of one fee.*

CHAPTER VIII.

No. 5.—Charter of Robert de Chauz.

ROBERT DE CAUS—DE CAUCIS.

GENEALOGISTS appear to have satisfied themselves with guess-
ing, instead of investigating, the facts pertaining to the history
of this baron; and the consequence is not satisfactory. Yet
there exists many facts which might lead to a discovery, for
this is quite clear, that, although not the holder of great
manors, we find the first Robert de Cauz in high company very
shortly after Domesday, signing the Foundation Charter of
Lenton next after the Earls of Leicester and Northampton, and
Hugh de Grentmesnil, Sheriff of Leicester, and before all the
great Nottingham and Derbyshire barons, the Burons, the Fitz-
Ralfs, and. the Avenels. Of course there was some reason for
giving this consideration, and it is probably to be found in his
near relationship to Hugh de Grentmesnil, whose guest he
probably was upon that occasion.

Now, turning to the Grentmesnil pedigree, we find that all
those personages named were closely related. Robert, Earl of
Leicester, was son-in-law of Hugh de Grentmesnil, and Simon,
Earl of Northampton, was closely related to his mother; and
one of his aunts married William de Say, of the family of
Avenel, and another Robert de Curci; and the question
immediately arises, was this name Robert de Curcis identical
with that of Robert de Curci? This seems very probable,
for a final s is frequently dropped or adopted, and both families

spelt their names in very much the same manner. Chauces is very near Chauci, or Chaucis, and Kawcis, or Kwarces. Other forms occasionally used are still more like it. These are the forms in which both 'the Cauz family and that of de Chaworth usually spelt their names in the earlier charters we possess; but no name, perhaps, has been subject to such exquisite torture of misspelling as this. It would not be difficult to enumerate above a score of different forms of it.

The first notice we possess is in the remarkable certificate of William, Earl of Ferrars, which proves that Henry de Ferrars enfeoffed the ancestor of Robert de Chaucis, who was then his tenant prior to 1088? At the same time, it may be noted that Galf Camara held two fees, which Robert fil Ralf and Peter de Goldington then held. We next hear of Robert de Caucis holding land in Wragby, Lincolnshire, in 1112-14 (four carucates and five bovates, and one-third of one), apparently with Goisfridus de Hanselin, who would appear to be living as late as the 26th Henry I., since, it is alleged (?) that he fought at the Battle of the Standards. This is unfortunately the only reference to the Hanselin family in this document. (See Mr. J. Greenstreet's edition, page 16, line vii., of the facsimile, 11 of the translation.) Mr. Chester Waters, in his edition of this important document, states that the one was son, the other son-in-law, of the Domesday Lord, Goisfred de Hanselin, or Ascelin. But, unfortunately, though so very positive, he adduces no proof whatever in support of his assertion; and the document, presently to be quoted, seems positively to contradict it. It has been contended that Robert de Calz succeeded to a part of Geoffry de Hanselin's estates, but we have no proof that the Geoffry of 1114 was not him of 1086, and certainly Ranulf de Hanselin did not succeed until a few years, at most six or seven, after the Battle of the Standard. That there were two Goisfred de Hanselins seems to be a mere assumption on the part of Mr. Chester Waters.

In the first great Roll of the Pipe, we find some very important entries relating to this knight. £226 was paid upon the pleas of G. de Clinton for the land which Robert de Calz obtained with his mother, and 200 marcs besides, that the king might exonerate him from certain pleas at Blythe; and, with Walter his son, he paid 100 marcs of silver, and one of gold, for a grant of the land of Leowin Chidde, that is, Leowin the younger. In Derbyshire, Lewin Cilt held Sapperton and Breaston at Domesday; but neither of these manors are concerned in this entry. The land which he obtained with his mother, it is generally taken for granted, was the twelve and half fees of the Honour of Goisfred Ascelin. We find some colour for this statement in a Pipe Roll of 14 Henry II., where this number is deducted from the holding of Ralf Hanselin, and said to be in the king's hands, possibly only deducted for the purpose of dower; but it may be, perhaps, that the lands of this lady were a portion of Roger de Busli's. In the present Roll, Ralf Hanselin accounts for 200 marcs of silver, and one of gold, for a relief for his father's lands, of which he obtained only the twenty-five fees. Now, it would appear from the records of the Knights of St. John of Jerusalem (Monas., Vol. II., page 534), that Amicia was the name of this lady, and that she was with Robert, her son, a benefactor of that foundation. But possibly this was a second, or even a third, Robert de Calz, for the number of the barons of this name is by no means clear.

It would appear from the charter relating to the land of Galfry de la Fremunt, the chief tenant of Robert de Calz, that his mother must, in some way, have been connected with the family of Roger de Busli, for in the reign of Henry I. Jordan fil Halan, Lord of Tuxford (no doubt his nephew), granted the whole of the manors held by this tenant of Robert de Calz to him; and the fine of 200 m. which, according to the first great Roll of the Pipe, Robert de Calz accounted for at Blythe, was probably in respect of these fees. Thoroton, Vol. III., p. 213, asserts that this Jordan fil Alan was sheriff of these counties the previous year. But that may be an error, for Ivo de Heriz answered for the rents of the manors of the county, and for the old farm of the same. The late Mr. Eyton has endeavoured, unsuccessfully it appears to the present writer, to prove that William Peverel was the earlier sheriff; but there seems every reason to believe that Ingelram, Lord of Alfreton, was hereditary sheriff of the two counties. He may, indeed, have succeeded Jordan fitz Alan, who was his cousin, in the sheriffdom, but there seems to be no proof of it. At any rate, his descendants enjoyed the sheriffdom for four generations. The first great Pipe Roll shows that, for some cause, Ranulf fil Ingelram had been disseized, for he paid a small fine of ten marcs to repossess his lands ; and possibly during this period a deputy had acted for him. As before noticed (page 94), Jordan fil Alan was probably identical with Jordan de Busli, also mentioned in this Roll ; and it would seem that he must also be identical with that Jordan fil Ernald, the brother of Roger de Busli, through whom the Viponts claimed. This discrepancy in the name of Jordan's father was probably well known in the reign of King Henry III., when the great Busli suit was in issue ; and it will account for the omission in that suit of the Christian name of Jordan de Busli's father. Probably Roger de Busli had brothers of both names. It is to be hoped that this clue, when worked out, may throw a clearer light upon the history of the family.

It would seem from the expression, " Robert de Calz received this land with his mother," that he obtained her marriage and dower (twelve and half fees being exactly one-third of Goisfred Hanselin's fees), and this fee, notwithstanding its illegality, remained in the possession of the family of de Calz. It is nearly certain from this that this lady was the widow of Goisfred Hanselin. But Robert de Cauz was probably her son by her second husband (who was probably Robert de Caucis, the witness of Lenton Priory, and afterwards the Forester of Nottingham). That Robert de Calz was descended from the Forester is stated in several records, but although the mode of descent is given, it is not stated whether he was heir on the part of his mother or of his father. We have proof that, during the reign of Stephen, Robert de Caus enjoyed the land, for which he had fined, for in 1139, Alexander, Bishop of Lincoln, in founding the Priory of Hafreholm, gave satisfaction to Ralf Hanselin and Robert de Caus, the Lords of Stretford (Monas., Vol. II., p. 792, old edition).

In 4 John (R.C.R. No. 17), Matilda, widow of Robert de Caus (he left a widow, as appears by the Lady's Roll of 33 Henry II., who was the daughter of Richard Basset, Chief Justice of England ?) sued John de Caus for her dower in Kilburn, Bliburc, and Redburn, in the County of Lincoln. It seems incredible that this lady could have been the widow of the lord of 33 Henry I., but it is just possible.

John de Caus contested the claim with regard to Bliburc. He was, therefore, clearly the son of a previous marriage, for his mother was already endowered therein. This leads us to a mass of information somewhat difficult of digestion; but it opens up the possibility of the mother of Robert de Calz having had no inheritance which could descend to her son, she having been the second wife of both her husbands. (See more of this matter hereafter in No. 7, Charter of Ralf fil William de Walichville.)

Turning to the Lincolnshire Roll, we find that in 1112-4 Gilbert de Calz (fo. 3) held 5 bovates in Ounebi, 4½ in Bliburc, 4 in Wadingheheim; and that Gilbert fil Gocelin held 7 bovates in Bliburc, land in Harpswella, Glentworda, Ingham, Cotes, Hacktorn, Ounebi, which Robert de Haia held of him; sum, 10 carucates and 2 bovates.

Nigel Albini also held land in Bliburc.

From the same Roll (fo. 4) we find that Gilbert, son of Goscelinus, held other carucates in Redburne, Botelsford, Asebi, Scallibi, and Wadingham; together, 11 carucates and 3 bovates. It would seem, therefore, that both Robert, and John de Caus, his son, inherited the land of Gilbert fil Goselin of the time of Henry I. He was a great landowner; and we find many other entries in this Roll relating to him.

(Fo. 8.) Robert, the Bishop of Lincoln, of the barons of the king, holds in Stowa 1 carucate of Gilbert fitz Gocelin. (Fo. 9.) Gilbert fil Goscelin holds in Viflingeheheim 6 carucates; (fo. 10) in Teflesbi, Wiflingeham, and in Normanabi. (Fo. 15.) In Chelebi Gisl de Chaz holds 2 bovates, and in Harburc, Neosum, and Brochesbi. (Fo. 18.) Gisl, son of G. and Geradus, in Sticheswold. (Fo. 19.) Gislebertus, son of Gocelinus, 2 carucates in Welletuna; Freschena (fo. 20) in Marchebi 4 bovates, Maltebi 4 bovates, which Walter fitz Ragmerus holds; (fo. 22) Houtona, Bekering, Snellesland, Reresbi, Suntorp, and Bleseby; (fo. 24) in Aschi, Sumerdibi, Tedford, Hamrigheheim, and Endrebi.

There was a Robert de Caus of Ingwardine who died without issue in 1187, leaving a brother Alexander, but his widow's name was Lucia. In 1226 Alexander demised to Wm. de Creddon.

The Pipe Rolls of Henry II. show distinctly what was the lands for which Robert de Cauz paid so large a sum at the time of the first great Roll of the Pipe, but they do not show under what right of succession he obtained them ; and it is probable that this was one of the high-handed acts so common in that age. It would seem that it was not his mother's inheritance, though it may have been his grandmother's ; but it is probable that it was part of Goisfred Hanselin's. He certainly enjoyed part of it in his mother's lifetime (as the Lincolnshire Rolls prove), in conjunction with the true heir ; and he paid a relief for his inheritance the same year. All this forms a story so complete, that but little doubt is left as to its true meaning ; but if any doubt remained, it would be clear, from the notices in the Roll of 14 Henry II., when the entire inheritance of Ralf Hanselin is acknowledged to be $37\frac{1}{2}$ fees, and $12\frac{1}{2}$ or one-third are still stated to be in the hands of the king, although another part of the same Roll discloses the fact that Robert de Chauz was holding them, perhaps as farmer: we do not know when his mother died, and the excuse for his doing so may have remained for a long period.

Ralf Hanselin died before 18 Henry II., for Thomas Bardolf his heir then paid scutage for 25 of his fees. There are several entries upon the Pipe Rolls which are worthy of consideration, if only to show the position of Robert de Calz. Thoroton seems to deny that he was ever forester, and would imply that William de Peverel held the office, because in the first Roll of the Pipe, which he erroneously asserts is the date of 1 Henry II., he then accounts for £23 6s. 8d. for the pleas of the forest ; and when his estate was in the hands of the king the sheriff accounted for £4 for waste of the forests ; and he assumes that the sheriff had the whole revenues and profits of them. But it by no means appears clear whether the first item has in fact anything to do with the pleas concerning the forests, or at any rate with the especial office of the forester. The ordinary pleas of the Crown were called pleas of the forest because the king frequently heard suits whilst hunting, and the payment of £4 may well have been for some forest trespass of the exiled baron. Thoroton (or rather Serjeant Boun, for he is the author of this account) has overlooked a most important entry, which shows distinctly that Robt. de Chauz held the office (in a Pipe Roll of 3 Henry II.) "Robert de Chalz renders composition of 20 marks for the ministry of the forest," and he may have held the office much earlier, possibly at the date of the Lenton charter.

It would seem that Robt. de Cauz was not a favourite with King Henry II., for in the 6th of Stephen he included in a charter to the Earl of Leicester, which may be genuine, though it was never acted upon, the estates of Robert de Chalz; and 10 Henry II. Robert de Calz, besides paying £20, paid 40 m. de misericordia. Evidently he was now in some fresh trouble. Nor does he appear to have recovered his position, for in 13 Henry II. Rich Ursel, his tenant, pays for him ; and in 14 Henry II. Reginald de Lucy pays £20 de censu foresta, and owes £15 16s. de misericordia of Robt. de Calz : and he is charged 12½ marks for scutage, so that Richard de Lucy was evidently farming the inheritance.

In 16 Henry II. there is a curious entry. Matthew and John render composition of £8 for having the goods of Stephen the forester. The following year Ralf Hanselin was dead, and probably Robt. de Calz. The king excuses the balance of his fine, £15 16s. The sheriff accounts for £18 9s. 6d., the pleas of the forest, and £80 28s. 8d. for wastes and assarts for the counties of Nottingham and Derby.

In 21 Henry II. there is an entry Fridbor de Terra, Robert de Chaucis.

In 23 Henry II. Ralf fitz Stephen pays £20 de censu foreste in Sherwood. Was he in any way connected with the forester Stephen who died only a few years previously?

In 9 Richard I. Ralf fitz Stephen paid £12 scutage for the fees of Robert de Calz, by which time he had married the heiress ; and we know that he was dead before the 6th of King John, for that year Godfrey de Albini fined with the king for £1000 for license to marry Matilda de Calceto, the widow of Ralf fitz Stephen ; and he modestly adds, " si ipsa voluerit eum accipere." It would seem that his modesty was not at fault, for there is a subsequent entry in the Roll showing that no payment was made ; the king forgiving the debt.

The previous year the Earl of Huntingdon was ready to account for 1,000 marcs that his son Henry should marry Maud de Cauz with her inheritance. In 15 Henry III. Stephen de Seagrave bought and paid for the marriage of Emma de Caus, a widow, for his son John.

The history of Ralf fitz Stephen is involved in obscurity, and we must probably look to the history of the Caus family to unravel it. Turning to the Lincoln Roll, 1114, we find that Gilbert fil Goisfridus de Calz held lands in the manors of Westletebi, Sunetorp, Snellesland, and Reresby, all in the wapentake of Wengho, and, curiously, Simon fil William de Kime held land in all these places. Now, from the Kirkstead Chartulary (Cott. Lib. Vesp. E. xviii.) in 1163, we find a Simon de Cauci attested a charter of Philip de Kime, son of Simon, and from this chartulary we can draw a complete pedigree of this family of fitz Stephen for several generations, all of them dealing with those four vills of Gilbert de Calz.

(Fo. 109.) Stephen fitz Herbert, Camera of the King of Scotland, granted land in Sunetorp and Snelland to the Abbey, to which Philip de Kime was a witness.

(108 C. V. L.) Stephen de Wikekebi (no doubt the same person) granted the manor of Westletebi to the Abbey, to which Robert de Curli, Hugo de Ard, and Hugo fil Com de Warwick, with Simon de Kime were witnesses. This charter, from the name of the last witness as well as from its place in the chartulary, clearly precedes the other in point of date.

Simon de Wik Camera granted land in Wik (*tempe* Lambert de Scoteny), in which he mentions Robert his son ; attested amongst others by Roger de Derby and Drogo fil Ralf. William, Earl of Warwick, confirmed this charter, Robt. de Curli, Hugo de Ard, Hugo, brother of the Earl, and Simon de Kime attesting.

(Fo. 109.) William fitz Eudo gave a toft in Reresby, to which Stephen Camera was a witness (at fol. 23 of the chartulary there is mention of a Eudo fil Gocelin). Stephen Camera with Ralf Tany (?), Drogo Freville attested the charter of Martin Martel of Canwich. (Gilbert de Gant's manor.)

(Fo. 109.) Ralf fil Stephen de Hoiland gave a toft in Snelland.

(Fo. 117.) Ralf fil Stephen de Wibreton gave land in Snelland and Sunetorp. The names of the vills out of which these grants were made, clearly show that the families of Wikekebi, Wik, Hoiland, and Wibreton were identical.

Ralf fil Ralf de Wibreton confirmed with Stephen and Roger his brothers.

23

(Fo. 119*b*.) Helto de Snelland gave land there of the fee of Rad de Hoyland and of William fil Gauf, which Robert Marmion attested. He himself attested a charter of William fil Eudo concerning Reresby. Ralf fil Stephen confirmed Helto's charter, so did Ralf fil Ralf fil Stephen de Hoiland, obviously the same family, Wibreton lying in Holland.

The William fitz Ralf mentioned in Helto's charter was probably William fitz Ralf (de Hardwick) of Steynesby, who was a son of Pagan de Scapwick. Sir Jocelyne de Scapwick attested his charter. Ralf fil Stephen de Hoiland attested Robt. de Carlton's charter.

(F. 116.) We have a Robert fil Stephen Camera of Wikenhebi, who also granted land in Westletebi.

There is no doubt whatever that Ralph fil Stephen was closely related to the chamberlain or Camera of Henry II., to whose office he ultimately succeeded. In 3 Henry II. it is stated that Ralf fitz Stephen paid in the Camera of the king by the hands of Warin fitz Gerald, who about the same time ceased to hold the office, as we have seen Robt. de Chalz accounted this time. We have met with a Geradus before in Lincolnshire holding land in conjunction with Gilbert de Chalz. Now, if Chalz or Caucis is the same name as Cauci, this Warin was probably the son of the former. Guarin fitz Gerald was one of the witnesses of Henry II.'s charter to the Earl of Chester just mentioned, and Robert de Curci Dapifer or Camera was also a witness to it, though what his relationship was we do not know, and we find at Belvoir Castle two charters of Guarine fitz Gerald, Camera Regis, and Alice de Curci his wife granting land to Fulc Breant and Henry de Codham.

Robert de Curci was in England in the time of William Rufus, for he attested his charter to Lincoln. Surely he was the witness of this charter to Lenton only a few years later, and uncle of Robert de Cauz of Nottingham. But we must resort to Norman records for an account of the family in order to explain their connection with the Grentmesnils.

They were seated at Curci sur Dive, and were neighbours and allies of the great families of Giroe and Grentmesnil. Ordericus gives an account of their warfare with Robert de Belesme, the exiled Earl of Arundel. Richard de Curci was then an old man like the great Hugh de Grentmesnil, but they both acted vigorously in this campaign, and in no small degree contributed to its success. Ordericus as usual gossips about the relations between the two families, and tells us that Robert de Curci had married Rohaise, daughter of Hugh de Grentmesnil, and that she had borne him five sons. We learn also from Ordericus that the seneschal or Camera of Hugh Grentmesnil was one Gerald by name, who was governor of the Castle Neufmarche. Probably Warin fitz Gerald, who married Alice Curci, was his son. We know that Robert de Cauz had a sister Alice, for she held a fee of him, as appears by the first part of the reign of Henry II., of new feoffment. Richard de Curci attested the charter of William the Conqueror to the Abbey of Marmoutiers, confirming the grants of Nigel de Constantine (Albini) to that institution. Again, with Hugh Grentmesnil, he attested the charter of the king to the Abbey of St. Stephen at Caen, and a few years earlier amongst the knights of the same Viscount St. Sauveur, granting land to the same Abbey is the name of Goisfridus fil Robert Venator, who may possibly be the father of Gilbert Chalz of Lincolnshire, for the suit of the time of King John shows clearly that they were all of one family, and this record his profession.

Robert de Cauz gave Doverbeck to Thurgarton Priory.

It seems very probable that the family of Iorz of Burton were a branch of this family, but still more clearly would it appear that the Chaworths are so. In the reign of Henry II. their name was spelt Chaucis, and in some documents relating to Marnham it was spelt Kawcs, which is as near the name Caus as a blundering scribe could make it, and utterly unlike the modern form of their name.

It is doubtful whether that Robert de Caucis who married the daughter of Ralf fil William de Waltville or Walichville was the founder or the intermediate ancestor of the house of Chaworth. The Red Book gives no intimation where the fee lay, and we can only judge from the context that it was one of Goisford de Hanselin's manors. Thoroton assumes that it was Marnham, but without any proof. It must not be forgotten that at Domesday the manor was held by Ingram, lord of Alfreton.

In 14 Henry II., the Pipe Rolls show that Robert de Chaucis paid 20s. for one fee to the scutage of that year, but there is no proof that Marnham was the fee referred to in the certificate of William de Walichville, and it would seem that John, the constable of Chester, whose claim to it could only be through the de Buslis Lords of Ingram's family granted the Church of Marnham to the Knight Templars, with whom it remained until the reformation of Henry VIII., when, of course, it fell into reformed hands. King John, in the fifth and sixth years of his reign, confirmed to Robert de Chaucis the manors of Marnham and Wadworth, which it was stated was the inheritance of William, his father, but these grants often lie, especially in King John's reign, and at this time probably the marriage of William de Chaucis with the ultimate heiress of Alfreton had taken place.

In 14 Henry III., William de Chaucis (son of Robert) acknowledged that he owed Alice, Countess of Auge, 55 marks of the fine made some time previously between them, and in 28 Henry III. the king confirmed the grant of the said Countess of Ewe to Robert de Lexington, of the custody of the whole land which was William de Chaucis' in Marnham. Upon the whole circumstance of the case, it would seem that Marnham, like Edwalton, devolved upon the Chaworths and the Lathams by reason of these marriages with the co-heirs of fitz Ralf of Alfreton, and the deeds so judiciously arranged by Thoroton must be displaced. The family very possibly held Marnham of the fitz Ralfs, though King John, for some reason, was induced to ignore them. It must be remembered that the Countess of Ewe had not yet re-established her claim to Roger de Busli's inheritance. The grants of William de Kawrcs, son of Robert de Kawrcs, to Radford, may have been made by the last William.

A Robert de Chaucis held one fee and a half of William Albini, Lord of Belvoir, in Leicestershire, of the old feoffment. Looking at the connection of the Cureis with the house of Belvoir (Roger Albini, the head of that family, *tempe* the Conquest, having married another daughter of Hugh Grentmesnil), it would seem to refer to that connection.

The only Ferrars manor that can be distinctly traced to the Caus family is that of Bradborne, which Lysons states, though he gave no authority, was held at an early period by the family of Caws or de Cauceis.

The church was given by Geoffry de Cauceis, in 1205, to the Priory of Dunstable, and he conveyed the manor to Godarde de Bradbourne, in the reign of King John. In all probability this Geoffry de Cauceis was the tenant for one fee of new feoffment mentioned in the certificate of Robert de Cauz, in 1—12 Henry II.

A manor in Brampton, called Caws Hall, was held by the family at a very early period. Lysons asserts that it was given *tempe* Henry II. to Peter de Brampton, whom he supposes was the second son of Maud de Caus. He, however, erroneously supposes that Adam (Peter's father) was the second husband of this lady, so that it is obviously a mere guess; besides, the dates show it is wrong, for Ralf fitz Stephen (Maud's second husband) was living in the time of King John. The manor was held under the Musards, and was probably an old holding of the family.

It may be asked why Hugh de Grentmesnil was a party to the grant of the Lenton charter, and it is difficult to account for his presence, except that possibly he was enjoying a hunting expedition. His only estate in the county was Roger Pictaviensis's manor of Edwalton, which he held in demesne. How it came to him does not at present appear, but his tenant, Robert fitz Ranulf de Alfreton, gave the church to Beauchief Abbey, and Thomas de Chaworth confirmed it.

Robert de Lathom, who is now represented by the present Earl of Derby, held the other half, the Earl of Leicester, whose ancestor had married the heiress of Grentmesnil, then being chief lord.

Ralf Basset, of Draiton, held one-third of the honour which Thomas de Chaworth held of him. It must be remembered that Matilde, daughter of Richard Basset, the Chief Justice, was the wife of a Robert de Cauz; how many there were in succession of this name as yet has not been satisfactorily determined.

There is yet much to be done in order to obtain an accurate account of the family of Curci. They were settled in various parts of the country, but are probably all of the same race.

At Domesday, Richard de Curci, who attested several of the Conqueror's charters, held Newham, Lecendon, and Foxcote, in Oxfordshire. He commanded at the Battle of the Standards,

and was succeeded by Robert de Curci, who founded the Priory
of Cannington, in Somersetshire, and who held the post of
Sewer to the Empress. This was .probably the witness to the
charter of Henry II. of the date of 6 Stephen already noticed.

It is not quite clear what relation he was to William de
Courci, of Stoke Courcy, Devon, who founded that Abbey.
Eton College has a charter of William Curci, the king's dapifer,
made to St. Andrew's of Stoke, for the repose of the souls of
Wm. his grandfather, and William his father, of a mill of
Norham, which he bought of Hugh Golafre, the witnesses to
which were Geoffry the Prior, Wm. Pantoul, John de Curci,
Jordan de Curci, Simon fitz Peter, Wm. de Reigni, Wm. his
nephew, Wm. and Durand Poher, Hugh Pincerna, Osbert de
Eston, and Wm. Chaudel. This knight is said to have been
the great grandson of Wm de Faleise and Geva. There is
something very wrong in the history of this family ; in one
account Wm. de Curci is said, in the time of Henry II., to
have ratified the grant of Avice de Rumeli, his mother, who
was the daughter of Wm. de Meschines,. brother of Ranulf,
Earl of Chester, to Ardington, in Yorkshire, of half Helthwaith
and Swindon.   In another, this lady is called Alice, and is said
to be the daughter of Robert de Rumeli, of Skipton, by Cicely,
daughter of Wm. de Meschines, and to have been the wife of
William fitz Duncan, Earl of Murres, and their daughter Cicely
to be the wife of Alexander fitz Gerald. Another record of
the 23rd Henry II. mentions that Alice, daughter and heir
of Wm. de Curci, then in her minority, was the wife of Warin
fitz Gerald, who enjoyed her inheritance. This must have
been Alice de Curci of the Belvoir charter, but there is probably
a confusion of epitaphs, as Mrs. Malaprop would observe. A
William de Curci was Justice of Ireland, *tempe* Henry II. A
John and a William were living in the time of Richard I.,
all of the Devonshire branch of the family.

FEES OF ANCIENT FEOFFMENT.

I.—*Galf de la Fremunt held two knights' fees ; he also held one
of new feoffment.*

NOTE.—He held lands in Kirkton Wileghby, Walesby, Besthorpe, and Birchwood, which his brother ultimately sold to
Hugh Bardolf. Matilde de Cauz, of her own free will, without

her husband, confirmed this grant as that of lands which the ancestors of the said Galfry held of her. Jordan fitz Alan (de Busli), Lord of Tuxford in the time of Henry I., gave to Galf de la Fremunt certain lands at Kirkton and Walesby, Willoughby, Besthorpe, and the wood of Muscamp ; and these evidently were not the Hanselin Manors sold by William, brother of Galf de la Phremunt, to Hugh fitz Ralf de Gresley, about the 5th year of King John. Possibly this grant will, when worked out, throw a light upon the entry in the first great Roll of the Pipe referred to at page 96, as the land for which Robert de Cauz impleaded at Blith.

Hugh fitz Ralf de Gresley who acknowledged suit of service for all these lands to Olivia, Lady of Tuxford, for his own soul and that of Agnes, his wife, granted them to Rufford Abbey. Both the Lady Olivia de Tuxford and Adam de Everingham (separately) confirmed this grant.

In the Rufford Chartulary, fol. 169 b., Matilde de Cauz describes the knight as Galfridus de la Freville (the name used by Gilbert de Norfolk, whom Emma de Belfou married).

2.—*Daniel de Creveceur held one and half fees.*

3.—*The wife of Robert de Arch held two fees.*

NOTE.—The family of de Arches held Grove of Roger de Busli and his successors, but little is known of them. One Robert held the estate at Domesday ; and Gerbert de Arches, *tempe* Henry II. The co-heirs of Arches, married Herecy and Rufus, and the heir of the last Eustace de Mortain, whose name and family are frequently found in Derbyshire records. The Herecys remained established for twelve generations, when Humphrey de Herecy, by Elizabeth, daughter of Sir John Digby, knight, left eight daughters and co-heirs, one of whom married Nicolas Denman, who succeeded to certain of his estates near Retford, and who was doubtless the ancestor of the great Lord Denman —the upright and independent Lord Chief Justice of the King's Bench—one of the great men of whom Derbyshire may be justly proud.

4.—*Jordan de Chevercourt held one fee.*

NOTE.—He was the son of Ralf de Chevercourt, of Carlton, in Lindric. He paid his relief for one fee there 11 Henry II., and is supposed to have been the grandson of Turold, the Domesday holder. Jordan de Chevercourt married the daughter of Ranulf fitz Ingelram, of Alfreton, whose great-niece married the son of Robert de Chaucis, of Marnham. Isabella, one of the daughters, and co-heiress of Jordan of Chevercourt, married Robert Furneus, of Beighton, and was ancester of the family of that place, whose ultimate heiress married Fitz Hugh of Ravensworth. Letice, another daughter, married Ranulf New march ; Mabel, a third, Ralf de St. George ; Aubrea, Robert de St. Quinten.

5.—*Thomas de Muscamp held one fee.*

NOTE.—This was doubtless the ancestor of Thomas de Mus-camp of North Muscamp and Carlton, who held them for one knight's fee of Robert de Everingham. The Muscamp pedigree is a very ancient one, but much confused on account of the divisions in their properties.

6.—*Robert de Daniel held one fee.*

NOTE.—Little seems to be known of this knight. A family of the name of Daniel or Daynet, were of Walkingham in this reign, Matilde Daynet or Daniel claiming the advowson in right of her ancestor against the Prior of Worksop, in 4 Ed. I. A great part of this parish belonged to Newstead Priory, and one of their properties gave rise to a curious decision—that a bastard could not, in law, be a vilain, because, presumably, a vilain must be a nativus of the lord. Throsby could find nothing in the place "suitable to the cravings of a hungry antiquary" (It seemed that he "craved" on horseback), unless it was " the azure limbs of certain naïads who ceased to lave them in the wave," whilst "the rosy band of smiles and loves going hand in hand, the Graces danced." All this, with much more of the sort, he beautifully describes in poetry. As he did so little for Thoroton as an antiquary, it is fortunate that something can be said in his praise as a Poetaster.

7.—*Ralf de Hamerwych held one knight's fee.*

8.—*Ralf fil Geremund held half a knight's fee.*

This half fee was in Oxcroft and Alvaston, in Derbyshire. His descendants granted them to Dale Abbey. (See Note to Hubert fitz Ralf)

9.—*Robert de St. Peter held half a fee.*

10 *and* 11.—*Ralf de Clapole and Ralf de Budington held one fee.*

Galf de Clapole attested the charter of Hugh fitz Ralf at Bingham, of land in Sibthorpe to Wm. fil Wm. de Selston, the first year after the election of de Langham to York.

12.—*Robert de Bellocampo held half a fee.*

KNIGHTS' FEES OF THE NEW FEOFFMENT.

13.—*Galf de Lefremunt held one fee.* (See No. 1.)

14.—*Galf de Cauz held half a fee.*

It is not clear where this lay. The author's index to Thoroton produces no Galfry; but Lysons gives a knight of this name, who is probably the same who held Bradborne under the Ferrars family, who in King John's reign gave the church to Dunstable, and conveyed the land to Godard de Brabourne. The name seems to have been spelt Caws and de Cauceis, exactly as the Chaworth family at this period spelt their name.

15.—*Richard Ursel held half a fee.*

In 11 Henry II. Robert Ursel answered for the debt of his lord, probably as seneschal.

16.—*Aliz, sister of Robert de Cauz, held half a fee.*

Unless this lady is Alice de Curci, wife of Warin fil Gerald, nothing is known of her; but that is hardly likely, since she was, by one account, in her minority quite a dozen years later. It is very unusual to find a female holding a knight's fee, and this is the only instance in Derbyshire Rolls, except the case of the widow of Robert de Arch.

And in his own demesne Robert de Cauz held 1 fee.

LIST OF TENANTS OF ROBERT DE CAUZ.

3.—Arch, widow of Robert.

12.—Bellocampo, Robert.

11.—Budington, Ralf.

14.—Cauz, Galf.

16.—Aliz, sister of Robert.

4.—Chevercourt, Jordan.

10.—Claypole, Ralf.

2.—Creveceur, Daniel.

6.—Daniel, Robt.

1 & 13.—Fremunt, Galf de la.

8.—Geremund, Ralf fil.

7.—Hamerwych, Ralf.

5.—Muscamp, Thomas.

9.—St. Peter, Robert.

15.—Ursel, Richard.

CHAPTER IX.

Ro. 6.—Carta Hubert fitz Ralf.

THE BARONY OF HUBERT FITZ RALF.

It may appear presumptuous to brush away summarily all that has hitherto passed current as history of the family of this baron ; but, as in many other instances, a strict adherence to truth renders it absolutely necessary. The Derbyshire historians, as they have done in the case of Robert fitz Ranulf, the sheriff, have mistaken the family of this baron, and here they have confused it with his mother's. It has always been confidently asserted that he was a member of the family of Rye, and proof has been offered in the shape of a strong inference which arises, it was supposed, from the fact that Hubert fitz Ralf of the Red Book bore much the same names (though the order is reversed), and held part of the same manors as the Domesday holder, and this fact has been supplemented by another equally as unsatisfactory and illusory—namely, that a branch of the Ryes, to which great family undoubtedly the Domesday Ralf fitz Hubert belonged, was settled in the Domesday Rye manor of Barlbro', and that they in the reign of Edward III. proved on a quo warranto that their ancestors had held a park therein from time immemorial. Strong facts admittedly, and perhaps far more valuable as proof than those which supports a very large number of the pedigrees which adorn Burke's Pedigree ; but, alas, both these inferential proofs are misleading, and both have absolutely no foundation to support the inferences built upon them.

The best account of the pedigree, as representing the views of Derbyshire historians, is to be found in the works of that eminent Norfolk historian, Mr. Walter Rye. As Derbyshire is somewhat out of his range, he evidently took the matter upon trust. He writes (page 5, of "An Account of the Family of Rye):—"Ralf de Rye (alias fitz Hubert) was the father of Ralf fitz Ralf, Baron of Crich *tempe* Henry I., who, by his wife Matilde, afterwards a Nun at Thurgarton, had (besides two daughters, one of whom married Geoffry de Constantine, and the other, Juliana, married Peter de Wakebridge [this latter is an obvious mistake for a marriage of the daughter of Hubert fitz Ralf, grand-daughter of Matilde]) a son, Hubert fitz Ralf, Baron of Crich, who died about 3 Henry III., having first married Edelina, daughter of William fitz Ralf, of Alward-deston (of a totally different family), and secondly Sara ; he died without male issue, leaving his daughters his co-heiresses."

"So ended the senior male line of the Derbyshire Ryes. But a junior branch was long settled at Whitwell, which was one of the manors Ralf de Rye held when Domesday was taken."

It may be best to get rid of the latter statement at once. Now, the Placita de Quo Warranto, which Mr. Rye quotes, does not prove, as he has taken for granted it did, that the ancestors of Ranulf de Rye, in the male line, ever held this manor, much less from time immemorial ; and it is perfectly clear from several suits in the Rot. Cur. Regis., and from other documents, that this park and manor were held by Robert de Meynel, descended from a Domesday tenant of Ralf fitz Hubert, and a knight of Hubert fitz Ralf of the Red Book, who died, leaving an only daughter, Isabella, some time in the reign of Richard I. The Pipe Roll of the 6th of that king shows that Sewell fil Henry, who married her, accounted for fifty marcs that he might have the custody of the daughters of Robert de Meynil (her grandfather), with their lands. This lady died s. p., leaving her aunts, the two daughters married to Matthew de Hathersage and Adam de Credling, her co-heirs. The Pipe Roll of 12 Henry III. shows that Mathew de Haversegg and Alicia de Credling paid 200 marcs for having seizin of the land which was Isabella de Meisnil's, consanguineous of the said Mathew and Alicia, which they held of the king in capite.

Now, it appears from the Rotuli Curiæ Regis, that Ralf de Rye who held this manor at the time of the Quo Warranto, before mentioned, obtained his share of it by marriage with the heiress of Credling, and it was his ancestors, the Meynils, who had enjoyed it from time immemorial. He himself, indeed, was not a Derbyshire, but a Lincolnshire, man, most probably of the family of the Domesday holder of the manor, but settled at Gosberchurch, in that county, from time immemorial. In fact, the union of the names was a pure accident. And it is also a fact that Hubert fitz Ralf derived his barony through his mother, and not through any Ralf fitz Ralf, Baron of Crich of the time of Henry I. This is clear beyond dispute from several charters in the Cartulary of Rufford Abbey, which still remain there. A copy is to be found in the British Museum. The Thurgarton Cartulary (Bodleian Library) shows that Hubert fitz Ralf's father was a benefactor of that foundation *tempe* Henry I., and that his mother, Matilde, afterwards took the veil there, when Hubert fitz Ralf himself gave, with her, the land which William fitz Gregory held in Scarcliff; and that Cartulary also shows that Hubert fitz Ralf called Robert Deincourt (a younger son of the founder) his brother, a fact which has always puzzled genealogists. The Rufford Cartulary explains this. It appears that Matilde (Hubert fitz Ralf's mother) was herself a co-heiress of Ralf fitz Hubert of Domesday (daughter or grand-daughter does not appear), and that she gave lands out of Scarcliff to Rufford Abbey for the good of the souls of Hubert, her son, and of Ralf fitz Eudo, her lord ; and the charter shows that this was a certain portion of her land (quendam porcionem terre mee) in Scarclive and in Languard, and that she made the donation in the name of Hubert, her son, and from him, for whoever would be her heir (faciam concedere et dare a filio meo Hubert, et ab eo quodcunc erit heres meus). Very clear words to show that it was her inheritance. The only puzzle is with regard to the word Languard. This must mean Langwith, which adjoined Scarcliff. If it refers to Langar, it will be found that the Deincourts held lands there, but that she had no estate in them. This charter was confirmed by another granted by Ralf de Aincourt and the Lady Matilde, his wife, for the soul of Ralf fil Edonis, and for the health of Hubert, his son, of the same land, with precisely the same boundaries, but with no mention of Languar.

This charter distinctly shows that Hubert fitz Ralf was not the son of Ralf Deincourt, and if Robert Deincourt was his brother, he must have been. Matilde de Rye's son, as was probably the case, by her second husband.

A third charter, by Geoffry de Constantine, confirms the same grant. A fourth, by Ralf Deincourt, confirms a grant by Robert Avenel out of the same place, and to this Hubert fil Ralf fil Eudonis, the baron of the Red Book, is a witness, or perhaps his father (the dates prove that there must have been two Huberts in succession). It is, then, abundantly clear that if there ever was a Ralf fitz Ralf of the time of Henry I., Lord of Crich, he must have been the father of Matilde de Rye, though in all probability it was Ralf fitz Eudo, her husband, who was so indicated, and who was dead before 1126, the alleged date of the foundation of Thurgarton Priory—a date which, fortunately, relieves Hubert from the stigma put upon this family by Dugdale and Madden, of identity with the thief who was hung by the partisans of the Empress at Devizes, an identity, however, which Mr. Walter Rye has clearly disproved. The only puzzling fact which arises from these circumstances is the date of these grants. The Pipe Rolls show that Hubert fitz Ralf was an infant as late as 14 Henry II., whereas the charters of the Deincourts concerning Scarclive, which were dated before 1126, were attested by him, from which it is certain that there were at least two Hubert fitz Ralfs in succession, and that the baron of the Red Book was not the survivor of the reign of Henry III., but his father.

The question now arises whether this Ralf fitz Eudo was a cousin of his bride, and himself a Rye, or whether he was of a different family. This is by no means an easy matter to determine. At first sight it appears very probable that Ralf fitz Eudo of the time of Henry I. was of the same family of Ralf fitz Hubert (or Eudo, these names being probably synonymous) of the time of Domesday. At any rate it is more probable than the supposition which has so long passed current in history, that Hubert fitz Ralf was so descended. I cannot but fear that Ralf fitz Ralf was an invention to bridge over the difficulty ; but there was another great family at this period

in Lincolnshire called fitz Eudo, from whom it is more probable
that he was descended.   This family were the ancestors of
the lords of Tatershall, and were distinguished by the sobriquet
of de Brito, no doubt adopted, as both were great Lincolnshire
lords, to prevent confusion between them and the Ryes of
Lincolnshire, the latter being a Norman family.

Following up this clue, the first we hear of the Britos in
Derbyshire is in the year 1102, at the foundation of the Lenton
Priory, when .Roger de Brito, a knight of Wm. Peverel's, gave
certain tithes in Walton and Calow, which he then held in fee-
farm of the king.   Now, this foundation was benefited by
Odo de Boney, who attested it next after Hugh de Buron, and
who was undoubtedly the son of Ralf fitz Hubert of Domesday.

Next we meet with a Ralf Brito of Annesley, who shortly
prior to 1161 founded the Priory of Felly, and endowed it with
the church of Annesley.   The date shows that he could not
have been the husband of Matilda de Rye, for he died before
1126; but he may have been his son by a previous wife.
When this foundation took place does not appear, nor is the
foundation charter known to be in existence.   The strong
probability is that it has disappeared for ages, and that
the delay in confirming this grant by the Pope, if this
Ralf de Annesly was the son of the husband of Matilda de
Rye, arises from the fact that Hubert fitz Ralf their son, or
probably his nephew, was yet an infant.   This foundation
was carved out of Matilda de Rye's Barony, and she must have
been a party to its confirmation.   In the account given
by Thoroton it is stated that Ralf Brito made this foundation
with the consent of his heirs, and afterwards it was granted
by Ralf Brito, and Reginald de Anesley, his son, to Worksop.
This part of the Rye Barony remained for centuries in the
Anesley family, although for a time the Stutevilles, who succeeded to this portion of it, affected to confirm their grants.
It would not seem that Hubert fitz Ralf himself very greatly
favoured this foundation, for he only gave it a small rent,
but the Pleslies, the Herizs, Barres, Insulas, and other great
tenants of the fitz Hubert Barony, all supported it, and so did
the Britos of Walton and Chesterfield, which tends to show
the connection between the two Brito families.

It is difficult to understand why this estate did not follow the rest of the fitz Hubert Barony, and it can only be accounted for by the supposition that Ralf, father of Reginald de Anesley, was a son of Ralf fitz Eudo (Matilda de Rye's husband) by an earlier marriage, and that this was given to him with her assent, and this was done in the reign of Henry I. The alleged Warsop grant being probably dated wrongly : looking at the dates, it is not very wonderful that all proof of the transaction is lost, and that we can only depend upon the mode of the devolution of the estates.

Derbyshire historians have always assumed that the fitz Ralfs were the male issue of Ralf fitz Hubert, whilst others (amongst them the learned Robert Eyton, the historian of Shropshire), have doubted whether he left any sons. The history of Lenton shows they were all in error upon this point, for one Odo or Eudo de Boney gave the church of Barton, half the church of Attenborough, and two parts of the tithes in Boney and Brad-mere to Lenton Priory, the foundation charter of which he attested, as was before noticed. As this was within fifteen years of Domesday, Eudo or Odo, who was thus disposing of part of the fitz Herbert Barony, must have been the successor, and in all probability was the son of Ralf fitz Hubert of that date. The reason why he only disposed of half of Attenborough was that it was all his ancestor enjoyed, Wm. Peverel owning the other half. Very shortly after this grant, Edward, and Ælis his wife, confirmed to Lenton what their ancestor Odo gave. This charter was attested by Ralf Barre Ranulf de Insula, and Hugh de Boney, and Ralf his son. It is confidently submitted that this Hugh and Ralf were also fitz Eudos, possibly Odo's brother and nephew, but almost certainly the latter was husband of Matilde, the sister of Odo, whose sister Matilde (possibly Aelis) was also the mother of the Edward who confirmed the charter of Odo. It is very easy to see why Ralf, the husband of Matilde de Rye, joined in this grant, for it remained her share of the Barony ; nor is it difficult to discover why Edward and Aelis confirmed the grant. There cannot be a shadow of doubt that this Edward and Ælis were of Saleby and Gunby in Lincolnshire, where they held part of the fitz Hubert Barony. We learn this from the Lady's Roll of 33 Henry II., when Leonia de Raimes, the widow of Robert de Stuteville, was then in the king's gift, heir to this inheritance, and stated to be upon her father's side a descendant of Edward of Salebir, and upon her mother's an heiress of the family of de Reimes, from whom she inherited the manor of Diham in Essex. She evidently thought her mother's family of greater honour than her father's, for, although an heiress of both, and chiefly through her father, she adopted her mother's name as her own. Her mother was the Aelis of the charter concerning Boney, and it is more than probable, she was the sister of Odo de Boney and his co-heir.

It appears, however, that this is a disputed point, for Roger Dodsworth has left a pedigree of the family showing that Edward de Salebir was not the despised person represented, but was no other than the great Edward de Salisbury, the Sheriff of Wiltshire, whose only positively known children were Walter of Salisbury, who succeeded him, and Maud, who married the great Humphrey de Bohun, certainly not a connection that one would expect to be ignored for the sake of claiming a descent from an unknown scion of the house of Reimes. Now it is tolerably clear that Edward of Salisbury was living in 1119, for he carried the Royal Standard at the great battle of Bremule, between Henry, King of England, and Louis, King of France, and Ordericus, speaking of him, says : "His approved integrity was of high renown, and never failed him even when fighting to the death," evidently pointing, not to a younger son, but to one of a long and well-tried career. He is again mentioned as amongst those who left the Blanch Nef after she had started on her last and fatal voyage, his age, no doubt, precluding him from willingly remaining with the drunken and riotous youths upon her. Now this was unquestionably the sheriff of Salisbury, and could have been no younger son, for the honour of carrying the standard in battle was of the highest, and if the first Earl of Salisbury was dead, his son Walter would have succeeded to the honour. Yet Mr. Chester Waters, and those who adopt his views assert, though without a shadow of proof, that there were two Edward de Salisbury's, and that the great Edward died in the time of William Rufus, an assumption that is absolutely essential to his argument. The author was recently involved in a rather too exciting correspondence upon this point in the pages of the "Academy," by Mr. Chester Waters, who challenged, not to say derided, the author's views upon the question, but that eminent scholar was

unable to meet the obvious retort that he had dimidiated
the real Edward of Salisbury to enable Roger Dodsworth's
theory to fit in with the dates, for it is impossible that Matilde
de Rye (not the before-mentioned Matilde, but her sister) could
be a second wife of the Sheriff of Salisbury, if he was the hero
of Bremule, because that lady, prior to 1107, was the wife of
Hasculf de Taney, by whom she had two sons, Rainold or Ralf,
the elder (who is lost to history), and Graelent, who, this Red-
book shows, held two fees of Hubert fitz Ralf of the old
feoffment, that is, he or his ancestor was enfeoffed before the
death of Henry I. If this was the first husband of the co-heir
of Rye, these sons would be the lords, not the tenants of Hubert
fitz Ralf, or, at least, would precede Leonia de Reimes in her
share of the inheritance. The heiress of Reimes (Leonia's
mother) married a second time in 1130, Pagan fil William de
Hocton, by whom she had two daughters and co-heirs, who
apparently ought to have shared in the inheritance of Diham.
One of whom, Matilda, was first the wife of Richard Grunbald,
Justiciar of England, and secondly, of Rich de la Peck; and
the other (Emma) married Ernald de Bosco.

It should be noted that whilst Mr. Eyton apparently adopts
the Salisbury pedigree propounded by Dodsworth, he doubts
the accuracy of Mr. Chester Waters' statement dimidiating that
sheriff, and adds this note to his copy of it, "so says Waters."
The real pedigree of the Salebir family is in great obscurity.
That the name is Salebir, and not Salisbury, as recorded in the
Lady's Roll, is tolerably clear from an entry in the Rot. Cur.
Regis concerning it.

Saleby was not an uncommon name in Lincolnshire, probably
it was a form of the name Saltfleetby, which is still called Salleby.
Philip de Kim, who was sheriff of Lincolnshire, 1169. granted
land in Suaby to Robert de Saleby. There was about the same
time a Hugh and a Roger de Saleby, and very curiously the
surname of this family was also fitz Eudo. It would appear that
two members of the fitz Eudo family married the two co-
heiresses of Rye, not an unlikely circumstance, since they were
all located in Lincolnshire.

It is a curious fact, established beyond doubt, that for some
reason neither the daughters of Ralf fitz Hubert, nor their
descendants, enjoyed the fitz Hubert barony during the life

24

of Henry I. This is clear from the first great Roll of the Pipe, which shows that it was then in the king's hands, and let to fee farm to several of the tenants, Gilbert de Mesnil, Ralf de Barre, and Robert le Lusors. The estate was then described as late of Odo fitz Ralf, who must have been the donor of Lenton priory.

Hubert fitz Ralf, after serving the king in the army abroad (he was with King Richard's army several years), became mad, and was aided by his relatives (so far as they could manage it) in squandering his inheritance. There is a curious record of a suit brought by the Attorney-General against Brian de Insula, who obtained a large portion of his estate. The Chartulary of Newstead, fol. 138 b., now at Heralds' College, has preserved evidence of the transaction in a charter from Hubert, granting all his interest in Scarcliff, Palterton, Langwath, and Risle, except what he had given to Anker de Freschville with Juliana, his daughter. Brian de Insula pleaded his charter in answer to the Attorney-General, who replied that Hubert fitz Ralf was *non compos mentis*, and that, by the king's command, there had been hue and cry to prevent any one from dealing with his inheritance. Brian de Insula was a judge, and in spite of this he seems to have won his suit, for he left these estates to his heir.

Brian de Lisle was closely connected with the fitz Hubert family. He was the son of Robert de Insula of Kirkby, a descendant of that Reginald who attested the fitz Hubert charter to Lenton. The de Lisles of Grace Dieu, according to Burke, claim him as a relation, but they were a distinct family. The connection with the Ryes is a very old one. Robert de Insula appears to have married a daughter of Berenger Todeni, the brother of Agnes, who married Henry de Rye, or, at all events, as the Lincolnshire Roll of 1114 shows, he succeeded to many Todeni manors; and Brian was also allied by marriage. For his second wife he married Gracia, the daughter and heiress of Thomas de Saleby, of Gunby in Lincolnshire, and with her enjoyed part of the fitz Hubert inheritance. (If Edward was of the Salisbury family, how was this Thomas allied to them?) We learn from Anker de Freschville's charters several facts which may eventually throw a strong light upon the history of the fitz Eudo family. It appears that no partition took place between the co-heirs of Ralf fitz Hubert of Domesday until the 33 Henry II., and that prior to this period those heirs had been allowed without partition to enjoy several portions of it. Probably there were two fitz Ralfs, and one was a minor, and it happened that they had each held certain portions which ultimately on partition were assigned to the other co-heirs; but this was not always the case, and it would seem that Alwodeston, near Derby, was enjoyed by the fitz Ralfs, and subsequently it came to the Freschvilles. Ralf Freschville, in confirming the grants of Hubert fitz Ralf to Derby, confirmed those of William fitz Ralf and of Robert his son, of the advowson of St. Michael's in Derby, and the chapel of Alwoldeston.

Domesday, as we have seen, shows that Ralf (fitz Eudo?) held Newton, Crich, and Scotchtorp of Ralf fitz Hubert at Domesday, but this family of fitz Ralf were quite distinct from that of Wm. fitz Ralf, the Norman Justiciary. Various conjectures have been made respecting this family of Wm. fitz Ralf, which require to be cleared up. It seems tolerably certain that Hubert fitz Ralf married and endowered his daughter Eveline, for he confirmed her grants to that foundation, though possibly they may have been made out of her own dowry. William fitz Ralf, her father, in some way was permitted to interfere with the inheritance of fitz Hubert, and to make grants out of it, but so did Ralf fitz Stephen, the king's chamberlain, who in 14 Henry II. would appear to have had the custody of Hubert fitz Ralf's inheritance. (See the Pipe Roll for that year.) It may be conjectured that both of them were descended maternally from the Rye family.

This William fitz Ralf of Alwoldeston may have been that person described as William fitz Eudo de Hibaldeston, to whom William de Lancelin, according to the Rufford Cartulary, gave a bovat of land in Walesby in free marriage with Cecilia his daughter. This William Lancelin was the son of Azelin Goisfred, Hanselin's great tenant. John and William de la Chause, who, doubtless, were relatives of Ralf fitz Stephen's wife, were tenants of the same place.

St. Michael's, Derby, was acknowledged to be the mother church of Alvaston in a suit tried in the reign of King John, and again *tempe* Henry VII., and William fitz Ralf, the Sheriff of Derby and Justiciar of Normandy, who dealt with it, seems to have disposed of it in favour of his daughter Matilde, the wife of Geoffrey de Salicosa Mara, for she gave the manor of Alvaston to Dale Abbey.

In a Roll of the Curia Regis (no date), one Isabella of Alwoldeston claimed two bovates of land in that manor against Galf de Salicosamara and Isabella fil Galfry. Nothing appears to be known of her family.

In Rot. Cur. Regis, No. 70, m. 4 (no date, but c. John), there is an Assize to determine whether the Abbot of Rufford disseized William fil Robert, Wm. fil Eudo, and Gaufry fil Ascelin, of common of pasture in Grimston-cum-Welhag, which he had of the barony of Robert de Cundy, and Gilbert de Gant. Soc. of Welhag was to be found in Grimston, Walesby, and other places, but Welhag is not mentioned in Domesday, probably Gilbert de Gant granted it to Rufford as part of Cratele.

In the time of Stephen, Gilbert de Gant made a grant to Rufford, reserving to himself the services of Hugh and Ralf, sons of Ralf fitz Remigius. Possibly this was Hugo fitz Ralf, who gave land which he purchased of Galf de la Fremont in Walesby, to Rufford, which Olive Montebegonis, daughter of Jordan fil Alan of Tuxford, confirmed.

This Hugh fitz Ralf was one of the barons who rose against King John. He married and obtained a great inheritance with Agnes, daughter and co-heir of Ralf de Gresley, by Isabella, daughter of Robert de Muscamp, a descendant of the senescal of the earl. More concerning him will be found in a note to Gresley and Wandesley.

There was a family of fitz Ralf at Wessington in Sallow, resident there *tempe* Henry II., and earlier, which puzzles exceedingly. They are only known by a series of Charters which are now at Belvoir Castle, Derbyshire records containing no mention of them.

Wessington and Oggeston were at Domesday divided between Walter de Aincourt and Ralf fitz Hubert.

Odo fitz Ralf gave Wessington to Darley Abbey, and Geoffry de Constantine confirmed it. Now Darley Abbey was only founded in the reign of Stephen, or very early in the reign of Henry II., and although the names Odo, Hubert, and Eudo are all the same, this Odo cannot be confounded with Hubert fitz

Ralf, who was an infant till the latter part of it, nor could he have been the donor of Lenton Priory, who was then dead. He was possibly the father of Hubert fitz Ralf II., of whom nothing is known.

The church of Crich was given to Darley by the Earl of Ferrars. By what right he possessed it it is difficult to see. It is, however, situated in no less than three wapentakes, and therefore its history is involved, and we may have but little of it. Portions may have belonged to different lords. Wessington was held (how does not appear) by the Abbot of Darley under John de Heriz in the reign of Edward I., whilst some of the family of Fitz Ralf continued under-tenants of the Abbey.

At Belvoir Castle is a Charter, s. d. of Ralf fil Simon to Darley Abbey, granting land in Wistanton and the land of Agenel, which Galfred Rural held, to which Robert de Oggeston was witness. It is sealed with a bird having its wings raised. This Ralf fitz Simon seems to have married Mabilia, the widow of Ivo de Heriz. She released her dower to John de Heriz in 10 Henry III.

27th Henry III. there is a Charter between Ralf fil Ralf of Wistanton and Mabilia, the widow of Ralf fitz Simon, and another Charter of the same to Darley Abbey, granting certain land, some of which was held by Mabilia, widow of Ralf, his father, in dower. To this Charter were the following witnesses : Robert de Esseburn, Robert le Vavasor, and Fulcher de Urtona, knights ; Roger de Thoc, Peter de Ulkerthorpe, Robt. Artheyk, Robt. de Oggeston, Walter de Merl, Will de Ley, Roger Clico, and Alex. de Lowe.

Then there is a Charter of Matilda, widow of Ralf fil Ralf de Wistanton, and another of 13 Henry III. of Robert fil Ralf of Winfield, which latter was attested by William de Glapwell and William de Normanton.

Henry fil John de Heriz confirmed to Walter, Abbot of Darley (1247-59), the land which they held of Ralf fil Ralf of Wistanton.

Walter, Abbot of Darley, according to the Derby Chartulary (Cotton. Lib. Titus C. x., fo. 39), granted to William fil Robert de Oggeston the land which Robert held of Ralf fil Ralf of Wistanton. This Robert was a Brito of Walton.

The same Cartulary contains a Charter of Simon fil Richard

(probably Ralf fil Simons' grandfather) granting to Magister Robert de Derby the land which Henry, his brother, held of him in Oggeston. Ralf, Abbot of Darley (1229-47) with the assent of the convent, conveyed to Robert fil Robert de Walton (Brito) and Cecilia, fil Magister Robert de Derby, for his homage and service, the whole land of Oggeston (Eggedeston) which the same Robert held of Ralf fil Ralf de Winstanton, to hold to the said Robert and Cecilia and their heirs, etc.

58 b.   Magister Robert fil Gode being sick, gave half the mill of Derby to the Abbey of Darley. This was in 1176.

Fo. 58.   King Henry II. confirmed the grant of Wachelin of Derby, and Goda, his wife, of the mill in Derby, which he bought of William de Heriz, and the grant of Ralf fitz Stephen and Hubert fitz Ralf of Childwell, Pentrice, and Crich. This William de Heriz, with Robert de Heriz and Wacheline and Goda de Derby gave Thurlecroft to the Abbey. This must have been prior to 23 Henry II., since William de Heriz died that year.

Fo. 88.   Letitia fil Nigel fil Baldwin de Derby confirmed the land, which Hugo fil Ralf gave with his daughter.

Fo. 110.   Ralf fitz Stephen gave Pentrice, Ripley, and Ulkerthorpe, which he held of Hubert fitz Ralf.

Fo. 132.   Robert de Oggeston fil Robert de Walton gave 8 marks to Dno Ralf de Esseburn. He married a daughter of Magister Robert of Derby, and held land of Ralf fil Ralf of Wessington.

Fo. 148.   Wm. fil Ralf gave the mill of Alwoldeston.

Robert fil Wm., the chapel of the same place.

Edeline fil William fil Ralf, land in Bolton, which Peter fil Roger gave to the canons.

Amelia, another daughter, land which Roger fil Reginald held.

Hubert fitz Ralf gave land in Childwell, Pentric, Ripley, and Ulkerthorpe, which his father gave, and Ralf fitz Stephen afterwards allowed (concessit). Walter, Bishop of Coventry, confirmed the grant of Ralf fil Odo and Gaufry de Constantine, made with the assent of Earl Ferrars, of Crich, Lea, Dethic, Ibol, Saunessey, Wessington, and Oggeston, and Salthorn to the same foundation.

To add a few Charters from Belvoir, possibly of value to the point, but certainly of great genealogical interest.

In 1275 there is a Charter of John de Heriz and Henry, Abbot of Darley, concerning Wistanton, attested by William de Oggeston.   The seal of Heriz : two lions.

Another of William, Abbot of Darley, to Ralf fil Henry Hert of Crich.

Hugo de Heriz de Grava to Robert fil Richard de Retford, vicar, and William fil Ralf, his kinsman.

John fil Galf de Plastow to the Abbot of Darley, 4s. rent from land in Aginhale in Wistanton, which Peter, his brother, held.

T. Ralf de Wistanton, Peter de Ulkerthorpe, Ranulf de Wakebridge, William Torcard, Alex de Lowed, Will de Ley, Jordan de Ybul.

In 1252 there is a Charter of Walter, Abbot of Darley, to Ralf fil Ralf de Wistanton and Matilda, his wife, to which were witnesses Ralf de Freschville, Roger de Eyncourt, Walter de Reibof, kts. ; Walter de Ufton, Robert de Oggeston, Will his son, Peter de Herthorpe, Ranulf de Wakebridge, John de Plaistow.

Then there is a Charter of Walter, Abbot of Darley, to Matilda, wo. of Ralf Wistanton, 1247-59 ; with two Charters of Ralf fil Ralf de Wistanton with the abbot, which Walter de Morley, Roger of Derby Clic, Jordan de Ybul, Wm. fil Ralf de Normanton, Robt. fil Robert de Aldwerk, Ralf de Winefield, Walter de Ufton, Will fil Ralf de Mston, Fule fil Fulc de Peton witnessed.

THESE ARE THE KNIGHTS' FEES ENFEOFFED OF THE BARONY OF HUBERT FITZ RALF OF THE OLD FEOFFMENT.

(It will be noticed that, unlike the other certificates, this charter speaks in the third person, from which it would seem that the Baron was a minor at this period, and that Ralf fitz Stephen, the king's chamberlain, who had the custody of his inheritance (and something more, for he presumed to make grants out of it), made the return for him.)

I.—*Robert de Meynil holds five fees.*

NOTE.—No doubt these fees were at Barlbro', Whitewell, Clune, Stretton, Egstow, and Hanley.

The first great Pipe Roll shows that Gilbert de Meynil then

held part of his lord's fee from the Crown at fee-farm. He
then accounted for £112 of the old farm (that is, arrears), and
£80 of the new. He also paid 20s. for the land of his brother,
and ten marcs for the king's license to marry. At the time of
Domesday, Robert held these same fees of Ralf fitz Hubert,
and as this lease carries the possession of the family back to
the early part of the reign of Henry I., it is most probable
(though there is no proof of it) that he was the Domesday
ancestor. There appears to be no doubt but that the tenant
here recorded was descended from Gilbert de Meynil of the
first roll of the Pipe, several charters showing that Robert fil
Robert Meynil of Barlbro' was the grandson of Gilbert. The
termination of his tenancy has already been mentioned in the
account of the family of Hubert fil Ralf.

2.—Galf Ridel held two and a half fees.

NOTE,—This knight was the son of Rich. Basset, the Justiciar
of England, by the daughter of Geoffrey Ridell, who perished
in the Blanch Nef, 1119, whose name he assumed, whilst his
descendants, as well as his brother, all adhered to their paternal
name. It has been pretended that the wife of Geoffry Ridal
was a daughter of Hugh, Earl of Chester, and undoubtedly she
obtained a grant of some portion of his property. It is most
probable that she was but a natural daughter, for had she been
born in wedlock she must have succeeded, instead of Hugh's
sister's issue, to that vast inheritance on the death of Earl
Richard in the year 1119. He was also drowned with his wife
in the Blanch Nef Ordericus, who gives a long account of his
father and his misdoings, distinctly states that Richard was
the only child of the late earl, although in another passage he
mentions a son Robert, who was dedicated to religion, and also
Otho, another son, tutor of the king's youngest son, but probably
they were illegitimate also. Ordericus notices that he had
several illegitimate children, and that nearly all of them came to
untimely ends. The mistake with regard to Geva Ridel has
arisen probably from the fact that in these lawless days the
stigma of illegitimacy was scarcely regarded as a bar to
inheritance, not at least by the Royal Family.

The Bassets long held the manor of Duckmanton of this
honour, which was probably the fee above-mentioned which

Goisfred (probably Ridel) held at Domesday   A charter of G. Ridel, is to be found in the Wolley Charters at the British Museum, which shows that his and the family of de Wiverton of Berneston were identical ; and that place, which came by descent to the Chaworths, is now one of the seats of Mr. Chaworth-Musters, of Annesley.

3.—*Robert fil Ranulf held two fees.*

NOTE.—This is probably the Robert fil Ralf referred to in the charter of Hubert fitz Ralf to Dale Abbey.

4.—*Galf Barre held two fees.*

NOTE.—These fees were in Tiversholt and Kirkby, and, like the Meynils, this family can claim to have almost a Domesday pedigree, for, like them, they farmed part of the barony at the time of the first great Roll of the Pipe. Ralf Barre then accounted for £12 9s. 4d. of the old farm.

Goisfred held Tiversholt at Domesday, and his name, or something like it, long continued a Christian name in this family. He was probably the Domesday ancestor of this family.

5.—*Graelent de Taney held 2 fees.*

NOTE.—The connection between this Essex family and the Fitz Huberts is a very interesting one. This knight was the second son, and probably the heir of Matilda de Rye, sister of the mother of Hubert fitz Ralf, and therefore his first cousin. She was Lady of Gunby, one of Ralf fitz Hubert's Domesday manors, and by her first husband, Edward de Salebir, she left a daughter and heiress, Leonia de Raines, who inherited her property.

Graelent de Taney succeeded to his father's inheritance in Essex, and at this period held 7½ knights' fees in capite in that county.

In 4 John, Ralf de Taney sued Robert de Taney for 8 bovates of land in Barneston, which he held of the gift of Ralf, his father. This probably constituted part of Graelent's holding.

6.—*Ralf fitz Stephen holds two fees of the fee of Hubert himself, as he, Hubert, asserts.*

NOTE.—This is a curious note to this tenure. It is stated to be of the fee of Hubert himself, as he (Hubert) alleges ;

in fact it would appear that for some reason Ralf fitz Stephen himself made this return.   Possibly Hubert fitz Ralf was already *non compos mentis,* or he may have been in his infancy.

There can be no question but that this was Ralf fitz Stephen, Camerarius Regis.   He married, perhaps subsequently, the heiress of Robert de Cauz, and in her right obtained part of the barony of Geoffry Hanselin, with the forest of Nottingham. He enjoyed these, however, but a few years, for King John granted the Honour to him whilst Earl of Morton, and he was dead before the fifth of his reign, for various offers of marriage are then recorded for the estates and the person of his widow, none of which, however, she appears to have accepted.

He appears to have been a Lincolnshire knight, and, as before noticed, to have held estates at Snelland, Reresby, Wikenhibi, Westladiton, and Wiberton, some of them probably of his wife's family, the Cauzs.

The Kirkstead Chartulary mentions several Charters of his and of Stephen, his father, Chamberlain of the King of Scotland. He appears to have had other sons, and to have been connected with a family named Fitz Eudo of Reresby, possibly Ralf fitz Eudo's own family.

7.—Reginald de Annesley held 2 fees.

NOTE.—These fees were of course in Annesley and Felley, and this knight must have been the son of Ralf Brito.

He would, therefore, if that father was identical with the son of Ralf fitz Eudo, Hubert fitz Ralf's father, be his nephew, or perhaps his first cousin.   This is not the less probable, since we find this fee to have been of the old feoffment.   It is of course possible that the father of Reginald de Annersley was a younger son of Matilda de Rye, as well as of Ralf fitz Eudo. The early portion of the Annesley pedigree is in great confusion, notwithstanding the great pains taken by the Heralds to perfect it for the Viscount Chaworth.   This work, which has been most kindly lent for the perusal of the author by Mrs. Chaworth Musters of Annesley Hall, is most valuable for the histories of other families connected with them, particularly that of the Bassets.

8.—Serlo de Pleslie held one fee.

NOTE.—This fee was Ashover.   He also held Glapwell of

William Peverel, and Pleasley also, from which place he took his surname. The latter is not mentioned in Domesday.

Ashover in the thirteenth century became divisible amongst the heirs of Serlo, one of whom married Willoughby, and the other Deincourt, the co-heir of the latter marrying Reresby, now represented by Sir George Reresby Sitwell, Bart., and the other Musters, now the ancestor of Mr. Chaworth Musters of Annesley Park.

9.—*Ranulf de Wandesley held one knight's fee.*

NOTE.—There seems to be some confusion between this family and that of Hugh fitz Ralf, who married the heiress of Gresley, who was also the heiress of Robert de Muscamp, and, indeed, it would seem that that Hugh must have been the eldest son of this Ralf, who, on account of the great inheritance he obtained by marriage, left this smaller one to his younger brother. Unquestionably, this knight was represented by his ancestor in the reign of Henry I. He or his son was living here in 22 Henry II., as we learn from the Pipe Rolls, when he paid three marks as his quota of the forests amerciments for that year. Thoroton says that a William de Wandeslie also paid two marks that year.

In the 12th Henry II. Orm de Wandeslia paid 10s. This is probably a mistake for Orm de Tanesleia.

In 25 Henry II. the Sheriff accounted for small sums received for the goods of Hereward and Hacon de Wandesley.

Ralf de Wandesley gave certain lands in Wandesley to Felley, which Nicolas his brother afterwards confirmed. Alexander de Wandesley succeeded, and Ralf his son succeeded him. 4 Henry III., there was a pardon granted to Henry de Estweit for the death of Ralf fitz Ralf de Wandesley. In 14 Henry III. the Prior of Felly brought an assize against Nicolas de Wandesley, Alexander fitz Hubert, and others, concerning certain fences. This Alexander certainly seems to be identical with Alexander de Wandesley; and as he was the son of Nicolas, this name Hubert was evidently used as a surname. This confirms the probability of the suggestion already made, that Hugo fitz Ralf was of the family of Ralf fitz Hubert of Domesday, and of his son Odo de Boney. We find this Hugh fil Ralf granting rents and lands in Wandesley, some twelve bovates, and twenty-four solidates of land, and eightpence rents to Stanley Priory. How could he do this whilst the Wandesley family undoubtedly remained in possession of their inheritance for at least fifty years afterwards, until, indeed, in 33 Edward I., the inheritance was divided between the co-heirs and daughters of the last Ralf de Wandesley, Joan the wife of William de Cressy, and the wife of William Folejambe of Gretton.

The Testa de Nevil states that Ranulf de Wandesley held Selston of Robert de Stuteville, and yet prior to this Hugh fitz Ralf had given a large number of bovates out of that place, some seven, together with a rent of 12s. which Nicolas de Wandesley paid him, showing that he was clearly his superior lord.

Selston had been the fee of Wm. Peverel, but Wandesley had belonged to Ralf fitz Hubert at Domesday. We can therefore only conclude that Alexander fitz Hubert and his ancestors, called fitz Hugh and fitz Ralf, were the descendants collaterally or direct of the Domesday holder. In Henry III.'s time, Ranulf de Wandesley, with his son Galfry, attested the charter of Reginald de Insula.

We find Alexander de Wandesley repeatedly attesting the charters of Robert le Vavasor of Shipley, and others, to Rufford, and sometimes as the first witness.

It appears from a subsidy Roll that a younger branch of the family held lands there in the 6th of Henry VI., in which time there was also some of the same name settled at Wingerworth.

Roger de Wandesley attested a charter of Robert de Tibetot's to Thomas fil John Foljambe concerning the manor of Elton, signing immediately after Thomas de Gretton. A copy of this charter is now at Belvoir Castle. It is perhaps dangerous to speculate, but the guess may be hazarded, that the family who appeared before the Heralds on their visitation of Derbyshire, holding a manor of this name in Darley, which at Domesday formed part of the king's manor of Metesford, then called Wandesley, are identical in origin with the Nottinghamshire family, but the connection between them has not been discovered, nor, except in the connection between the Derbyshire family of Foljambe, who were also called de Gretton, is there at present any trace of relationship. This, however, is quite clear—the same family held both manors, a very remarkable instance of a manor, at so early a period, being called after the name of its lord, that name being also the name of his territory in another county.

The conclusion to be drawn from this account is that the Nottinghamshire family were identical with that of Hubert fitz Ralf their lord, and that the Hugh fitz Ralf who married the heiress of Gresley was no other than the witness to Edward de Salebir's charter to Lenton. That charter was probably made not very early in the reign of Henry II. (he probably survived), for we hear nothing of Robert de Stuteville, who married his daughter and heiress, and the first we hear of his son is in 33 Henry II., when partition was made.

10 and 11.—*Hugo de Somery and Robert de Barton held half a fee.*

NOTE.—This half fee was probably in Barton.

12.—*Galfry de Cotestin held* 11½ *knights' fees. Ten of his own demesne of the new feoffment, which he obtained in marriage with the sister of Hubert, by fine made before the king.*

NOTE.—Part of this fee was in Barton. Robert, the son of Robert Cotestin, had an interest here in the time of Edward I.

A LIST OF THE TENANTS OF HUBERT FITZ RALF.

7. Anesleia, Reginald.		3. Ranulf, Robert fil.
4. Barre, Galf.		2. Ridel, Galf.
11. Barton, Robert.		6. Stephen, Ralf fil.
12. Cotestine, Galf.		10. Sumery, Hugo.
1. Meinil, Robert.		5. Taney, Graelent.
8. Pleslie, Serlo.		9. Wandeslie, Ranulf.

CHAPTER X.

No. 7.—The Charter of Ralf fitz William.

RALF fil William de Walichville held in the lifetime of King Henry I. (certain land) for the service of one knight's fee, and Robert de Chaucis holds it by the same service, which he obtained with the daughter of the said William, except two carucates of land, for which the king impleaded him.

NOTE.—This is a most puzzling entry, but one which, if it were fully understood, might aid in the solution of the difficulties attending the Cauz and Chaworth pedigrees. It can only be conjectured that this fee was in Walesby, which may be another form of Walichville; and probabilities point to this Rad fil William being a son of William Ascelin, chief tenant of Rad Anselin. There was a Ralf of Wadeland, in Walesby, who gave to the monks of Rufford the whole territory which John de la Chause of Walesby, and William, his brother, and other persons, held in Walesby. We have met with John de la Chause before, when he was sued by Matilde, widow of Robert de Caus. He must, therefore, have been the son of Robert de Caus, or, as he is called here de Chauces, by the daughter of William de Hanselin, or Lancelin ; and the gifts of Rad de Wadeland to Rufford must only have been a mere nominal sovereignty.

It is a curious circumstance that Walesby and other places were afterwards sold to Hugo fitz Ralf, who married the heiress of Gresley, and took her name. His origin, as we have seen, is in doubt. He may possibly be the son of this Ralf. This, too, would account for the puzzling charters of Matilde de Cauz rent of Chesterfield for that year, which was assessed by himself, the sheriff, by William Albini, and Simon de Patteshall, and by a jury chosen by the knights of the county. It would be of little use, however, to put in force the Archbishop's regulations with men like William Briwere, for in the same Roll which records his indebtedness is also recorded the fact that the king excused his payment.

There are two or three entries in the Rolls whilst William Briwere was sheriff, which would seem to indicate that he only farmed the town of Chesterfield for the king ; or else, that, like Derby and Nottingham, they were their own farmers. In 4 John (page 157), the men of Chesterfield paid two marcs for license to buy and sell stained cloth, as they were accustomed in the time of Henry II. Newark made a similar payment, and the following year Robert fil Peter de Brimington fined 50 m. for having the manor of Witington as his father held it by the charter of King Richard. This accounts for the objection of William Briwere to pay (or rather be charged—he never paid) £18 rent for that manor in the 6th of King John. This entry again shows that William Briwere's farm was later than the commencement of King Richard's reign, Peter de Brimington's farm being made probably in one of the years for which there is no Pipe Roll, and certainly before that of William Briwere. Several records of a later date show that this question of rent between Peter de Brimington and his descendants and the Briweres was the subject of disputes between them, though ultimately they were compelled to pay.

Derbyshire historians have lost sight of the family of Peter de Brimington, as indeed they have of many others equally interesting. It is difficult to conjecture their origin, but they were of great importance, and, like the families called de Duckmanton and de Glapwell, they were almost invariably parties to the charters of their neighbours the Britos, of Walton. Perhaps this was only because they were neighbours ; but looking at the importance attached to the attestation of charters by all who might by any possibility have any title by inheritance, it would seem that they were very possibly of the same family. Many charters relating to the de Brimingtons are to be found at Hardwick Hall, at the Foljambe's, at Osberton, and at others of the great depositories of Derbyshire Records, which will appear in due course in the Parochial portion of this work.

William Briwere's certificate dates prior to the first years of John, as the rate of assessment shows, and subsequent to the 6th of Richard I., for that year, or the latter part of it, was the first of his farm. This would therefore give the date of 7 or 8 Richard I. as that of William Briwere's certificate, so that it is one of the very latest in the Red Book; since the following year Archbishop Hubert Walters' new financial schemes came into force, for the purposes of which, no doubt, the Red Book was prepared. An account of this important measure of finance will be given in the next chapter.

𝔇edicated (by permission) to 𝔖ir 𝔈dward 𝔥enry 𝔖tanley, 𝔈arl of 𝔇erby, 𝔎.𝔊., 𝔓.𝔠.

Published by BEMROSE & SONS, 23, Old Bailey, London, and Derby; PARKER & CO., London and Oxford; and by WILFRED EDMUNDS, "Derbyshire Times" Office, Chesterfield.

THE FEUDAL HISTORY

OF THE

County of Derby:

(*Chiefly during the 11th, 12th, and 13th Centuries*),

BY

JOHN PYM YEATMAN, ESQ.

(Of Lincoln's Inn, Barrister-at-Law, formerly of Emanuel College, Cambridge, and F.R.H.S., &c.)

Author of "The Early Genealogical History of the House of Arundel;" "The History of the Common Law of Great Britain and Gaul;" "An Introduction to the Study of Early English History;" "The Mayor's Court Act, 1857;" "An Introduction to the History of the House of Glanville;" "A Treatise on the Law of Trades Marks;" "The Origin of the Nations of Western Europe;" "The Records of Chesterfield;" "A Treatise on the Law of Ancient Demesne;" "An Exposure of The Mismanagement of the Public Record Office," &c., &c.

The Author has the gratification to announce that he will have the assistance of

SIR GEORGE R. SITWELL, BART., M.P., F.S.A.,

who has made extensive collections for the Counties of Leicester, South Yorkshire, and Derbyshire, in editing the Hundred of Scarsdale.

MR. CECIL J. S. FOLJAMBE, M.P., F.S.A.,

will assist in editing the Hundred of High Peak; and other Gentlemen of high Literary repute will assist the Author in compiling other portions of the Work.

Price for the whole work TEN GUINEAS, if paid in advance; Large Paper Copies, Two Guineas extra.

To be published in sections of about 250 pages, Royal Octavo, each price Half-a-Guinea, or on Large Paper, 2s. 6d. extra. Two sections will form a Volume; each Volume, which can be purchased separately, will be complete in itself, with full indices, the whole work to be complete (if possible) in Twenty Sections; the subscription price will not be increased whatever the extent of the work.

subscribers' copies are distributed. 300 copies only will be printed, a portion of which only will be offered in England. Each copy will be numbered and signed by the author.

The first portion of the work will be occupied with Collections of Fees made from Domesday, the Pipe Rolls, the Testa de Nevil, Kirby's Quest, the Book of Aids, the Subsidy Rolls, and from other sources of the same character, in a form somewhat similar to that adopted by Major-General Wrottesley for the Staffordshire William Salt Society.

The parochial portion of the work will commence with the Hundred of Scarsdale, and after giving a history of its successive Lords, will contain that of the different Parishes and Manors, commencing with the Parish and Manor of Eckington.

The General History, with an introduction, will complete the work. The publication of this part is delayed in order to include all discoveries made during its progress.

The work will be embellished with illustrations of Castles, Ancient Manor Houses, Tombs, Crosses, with some modern Mansions ; and with many Plates of Seals and Coat Armour.

In order to meet the wishes of those who care less for particular History than for the contents of certain documents, some of which have not yet been edited, the author has determined to reprint certain portions separately, at a uniform price of 5s.

No. I.—THE DOMESDAY FOR DERBYSHIRE, is already published, 88 pages.

No. II.—EXTRACTS FROM THE PIPE ROLLS FOR THE COUNTIES OF NOTTINGHAM AND DERBY, with Notes, 174 pages.

No. III.—THE RED BOOK OF THE EXCHEQUER FOR THE COUNTIES OF NOTTINGHAM AND DERBY, with copious Notes (now in the Press).

No. IV.—THE FEE BOOKS FOR THE COUNTIES OF NOTTINGHAM AND DERBY, consisting of THE TESTA DE NEVIL, KIRBY'S QUEST, and the BOOK OF AIDS, with an explanatory account of each of them.

No. V.— EXTRACTS FROM THE SUBSIDY ROLLS FOR THE COUNTIES OF NOTTINGHAM AND DERBY.

No. VI.—THE DOMESDAY FOR NOTTINGHAMSHIRE is in course of preparation, uniform with the above.

And possibly some others will follow.

For the convenience of reference to the general Index of this work, the paging of these reprints will in future be identical with those of the Feudal History, of which they are a part ; the Pipe Rolls are paged differently. The printing of this Index, which is already partly made, will be deferred to the conclusion of the whole of these collected materials, and it will itself be a valuable work for genealogists, since it will contain, at one view, not only the names of persons and places, but the dates of all entries in the Rolls, and the localities relating to each name, and, where it is possible, dividing the group of each name into separate families ; in fact, under each name a skeleton Pedigree of the family will be given. It will thus be a guide for anyone desiring to trace the history of a family to all entries in certain of the public records relating to it. The Index will for this object be published separately in this series of extracts.

WORKS BY THE SAME AUTHOR.

THE HISTORY OF THE HOUSE OF ARUNDEL.

One Volume, folio, large paper copies bound in Morocco, Price Six Guineas; small paper copies bound in cloth, Four Guineas.

MITCHELL AND HUGHES, 140, Wardour Street, W.C.

The Author has the gratification to receive permission to publish the following very generous criticism of the First Part of this Work from the pen of Mr. THOMAS HELSBY, the learned Editor of the last edition of Ormerod's *History of Cheshire*, who writes :—

" I have had the pleasure and profit just lately of perusing an admirable book of the kind (Mr. Pym Yeatman's recent work on the Earls of Arundel), which contains a great amount of entirely original matter, with all doubtful points acutely raised, and well—almost intensely—argued, showing the zeal and pains which have backed up the learned Author's judicial powers and natural acumen. Of course, like all other history, this one of a family which represents in the aggregate a vast extent of Norman and English territory, is of a tentative character, but the valuable historical and genealogical matter is purified from the ordinary dross of such productions by having had the advantage of passing through a mind evidently thoroughly capable of reducing it into that state best suited for the critical reader ; although repetitions may be found numerous enough in works of this kind, they have their use in constantly keeping before the mind of the reader facts and arguments that less tenacious and ordinary minds would let slip."

And the following from Sir Bernard Burke, Ulster King at Arms, with reference to the whole book :—

" What a wondrous store of information you have laid up for genealogists in your grand ' History of the House of Arundel.' I am at every leisure moment poring over its contents."

Extracts from the "Manchester Courier" of 30th March, and 6th April, 1883 :—

FIRST NOTICE.

" In an age when the press teems with stately folios, lumbering weak-backed quartos, and even with octavos, of History, Genealogy, and Archæology, every one of taste and learning may be congratulated on the birth of a new folio of great originality and merit, and from the true historical standpoint. ' The History of the House of Arundel,' taking us back for a period of 1000 years, is one of those Works which may well have employed the valuable hours of a member of the learned profession to which the Author, Mr. Yeatman, belongs. The judicial faculties which he has brought to bear upon his subject have, on the whole, thrown so searching a light upon some long-buried points in national history, as well as genealogical problems, that the volume will be hailed by every scholar of unbiassed mind with the cordiality it deserves. ' The Early History of the House of Arundel ' is that of many of the most Historic Families in this country and in France ; and the bridge, which hitherto has been almost of the flimsiest character, is now fairly established upon the sound basis of numerous, if often fragmentary, facts—worked together, it may be, by some defective arguments, by much necessary repetition, dry and wearying details, but, on the whole, with a sagacity and acumen that redeems the work from all reproach."

"Nothing can well be of greater interest to the student than the genealogical connection of this kingdom with that of our continental neighbours and the old Duchies of Normandy and Brittany. Absolutely little of consequence was known (and this far from accurately) until the publication by the late distinguished Herald, Mr. Planchè, of his 'William the Conqueror and his Companions.' Sir Francis Palgrave in his Work was barred from going into all those details of history so necessary to a just appreciation of the connection of the ruling houses of England and Normandy, but his eloquent sketches of the Duchy will never fade from the memory of the cultivated so long as history holds its domain in the human mind. Other gentlemen of repute have since written upon this subject more or less fully ; but it seems to have remained for the present learned Author to unearth from the various archives of the French Republic, and from the great stores of materials in the Pipe Rolls and the Red Book of the Exchequer, and those in the possession of the Duke of Rutland and Lord Arundel of Wardour (extending in date from the reigns of the Dukes of Normandy and regularly down to the time of Henry III. of England), a large amount of original information, which, although of so fragmentary a character in many cases as to necessitate the utmost industry, skill and circumspection in using, has enabled Mr. Yeatman to give to the reader something approaching a sound and reliable Work on this interesting period of Anglo-Norman history."

SECOND NOTICE.

" To handle all the multitude of facts in this book (far exceeding in number, and often in abstruse significance any disclosed in the greatest *cause célèbré*), and to deal with them in a comprehensive manner, giving full effect to the numerous subtleties of meaning they often disclose, requires a grasp of intellect which can never be too fully appreciated. It is not surprising then if some should slip out of hand, and it would ill become the critic to score his page with black marks where there is abundance of merit so conspicuous to compensate for almost any degree of shortcoming, especially in a costly first edition which cannot easily very soon be supplanted by a second.

" In conclusion, the least that can be said of 'The History of the House of Arundel' is, that it is an admirable collection of facts ; and, if for this reason only, is very valuable, but its facts are skilfully arranged, and the learned Author has placed them in the most candid manner in every conceivable light before the reader, however laboured his efforts may occasionally appear ; and after the judgment and research displayed in this work, if he has failed to command, he has certainly deserved success. As a volume for the earnest student of both direct and circumstantial evidence, it is to be warmly commended ; and the many tabular pedigrees will repay the perusal of every one interested in the stream of history which connects so many of the past and present races with those of our own. We cordially congratulate Mr. Yeatman on the production of this admirable book."

From the " Bristol and Gloucester Archæological Journal," Vol. VII., Part I., a criticism by Sir John MacLean of Bicknor Court :

" The chapter on the settlement of the house of St. Sauveur, in the West of England, will be found of special interest to our readers, inasmuch as it gives the origin of many ancient families in the western counties, but the space at our disposal will not admit of our entering into details.

" To compile an authentic pedigree of one ancient family is no light task, but to grapple with those of many of the Norman nobility and trace their descendants respectively from original authorities is a work of Herculean labour, and Mr. Yeatman's Book, when completed, will form a monument of industry and patient research. He seems to be well acquainted with the several personages who come within his range, and, throughout all their shifting scenes, maintains, upon the whole, a firm grasp of their individuality. That there are many, and possibly important, mistakes in such a work would be unavoidable, and some of the statements made seems to us not to be vouched for by sufficient evidence ; nevertheless allowing for all these errors and shortcomings, the Work will prove a most useful contribution to English history and genealogy."

THE ORIGIN OF THE NATIONS OF WESTERN EUROPE.

Price 6s.

BURNS AND OATES, London.

" Every one must own the clearness of style, the cogency of argument, the wealth of illustration in the way of learning, the depth of thought, and the perfect indepen- dence with which the history of England is sifted. To many, perhaps most people, the criticism on the Aryan Theory, &c., will seem like an unpleasant revelation, but we strongly suspect it will be found far from easy to answer this book."—*The Metro- politan, 30th August*, 1879.

" Mr. Yeatman is one who has had the courage to combat popular opinion on Philology. Should the statements contained in the book lying before us be true, and to bear testimony without prejudice, we think it will be no light task to prove the basis of his theory to be untrue, the Oxford School of Philology is undubitably worthless, especially Max Müller's Aryanic Theory, which, in plain language, rejects the Mosaic Account of the Early History of Mankind, and holds up the Sanscrit to be the parent of all languages."—*The Auckland Times* (1st *Notice*), 26th *Sept.*, 1879.

A TREATISE ON THE LAW OF ANCIENT DEMESNE.

Written in Illustration of the Records of Chesterfield.

Price 3s. 6d.

WILFRED EDMUNDS, Chesterfield.

From Dr. Charles Cox's criticism of the "Records of Chester- field (Journal of the Derbyshire Archæological Society, 1885.")

" The work of transcribing, translating and editing these archives was entrusted to the capable pen of Mr. Pym Yeatman, and most ably has he done his task. The introduction is helpful and original, its only fault being its brevity."

" The work has been most ably done by Mr. Yeatman, than whom no one could have been found more competent for the task, and he has preceded the body of the work by a masterly, able and valuable historical preface, which adds immensely to its value."—*The Reliquary*, April, 1885.—By the Editor.

" This little book deals with a subject that is very interesting just now, and the records quoted by the Author, from documents relating to the Borough Courts of Chesterfield, are exceedingly curious. Mr. Yeatman gives some curious facts from Manor records and elsewhere, and his essay appears to us to contain some important facts which are well worth close attention from those whose special study it is to reconsider the history of land-holding in England."—*The Antiquary*, December, 1884.

Some Extracts from the Press relating to

AN INTRODUCTION TO THE STUDY OF EARLY ENGLISH HISTORY, &c.

The Metropolitan, 14th August, 1874.

" Old-fashioned people who believe in 'Mangnall's Questions,' 'Pinnock's Catechism of English History,' or in Hume and Smollett, will read this work with fear and trembling. We are not prepared to endorse all the views set forth in these pages, but the book is so immeasurably above the ordinary run of histories, which are mere repetitions of facts previously invented and judiciously arranged, that we must cordially advise every reader to study it intently."

Evening Standard, 12th November, 1874.

"This is a most original Work, overflowing with learning, and marked through-out with a complete mastery over the most minute details of this extensive subject. By far the most interesting portion of the Woik is the patient research shewn by the Author into the origin of the English language, and his dissertation on our Saxon literature, laws, and customs. Some of the most dangerous errors of Drs. Marsh and Latham are freely exposed, and with success ; with like freedom and success the hi-- torical errors of Mr. Freeman, Lord Macaulay, and Sir Edward Creasey, are brought home to their several authors."

The Press, Philadelphia, 20th November, 1874.

"The present volume is a remarkable example of original thought, historical research, philosophical deduction, and bold disregard of the merely traditional views of previous writers, who, taking too much for granted, have been content to travel in beaten tracks merely because they are old. To a large extent the Author ignores the claims of the Saxons as founders of either the language or the laws of England, and doubts whether, indeed, they had a distinct nationality. The Work is earnest and able."

The Law Review (English), Vol. III., N. S., p. 1139 (1874).

"Mr. Yeatman writes with all the spirit of a true antiquary. He has an ardent appreciation of his subject, and pursues it with a keenness and a zest known only to those who have for some time indulged in antiquarian research. His work turns up much fertile soil, and though we do not concur in his main views, yet we willingly recognise the general value of his treatise. Its main object seems to be to unearth those jural elements that lie deep at the base of our laws, and to assign them, if possible, to a British rather than a Saxon origin. In this view he is undoubtedly nearer the truth than those writers—and they are legion, including the great Blackstone himself—who ascribe a Saxon origin to our Common Law.

"His description of the influence of Roman jurisprudence on modern law indicates much literary grace and skill. It is clear that Mr. Yeatman is a rheto-rician, and a poet of no mean order. If ever he divests his thoughts from the Common Law, a boundless and more fertile field will lie before him in the domain of general literature. He certainly has all the qualities that constitute a vigorous writer. There is not anything improbable in most of Mr. Yeatman's views. His work indicates great facility of composition, and an intimate familiarity with all the leading arcana of Celtic lore."

The American Law Review, Vol. IX. (1874-75), p. 123.

"Mr. John Pym Yeatman possesses at least two qualities in common with the distinguished Englishmen whose name he bears—independence and courage ; without the former he could not have written, without the latter he would hardly have published, the extraordinary book which forms the subject of this notice. Mr. Yeatman has produced a remarkable book."

The Freeman's Journal (Dublin).

"Under this unpretending title Mr. Yeatman has given to the world a veiy valuable book. His introduction is not, as such works usually are, a mere transcript, more or less abridged, of the standard and approved authors on the subject. It is as remarkable for the boldness and originality of its views as it is for patient research and easy vigour of style. The author sets out with the theory that falsehood and exaggera-tion have mingled so largely with the writings of English historians, more especially since the Reformation, that it has become almost impossible to recognise the truth in its twisted, distorted form. He contends that it is not in the history of the Saxons, but in the ignored history of the Celtic race, that England has to look for the origin of all that she possesses that is valuable or noble—her language, her literature, her Common Law, and her Constitution. In the course of his very able work he boldly exposes the innumerable misrepresentations with which English history is underlaid, and advances many strong and ingenious arguments in support of the theory he has adopted. The book is characterised throughout by a patient, industrious, laborious, and patient research, and an honest desire to discover and declare the truth at all hazards and under all circumstances."

confirming the grants to Hugh fil Ralf of these same places. (See Galfry de la Fremunt, tenant of Robert de Cauz, No. 1.) The probabilities point to this Robert de Chauces being the ancestor of the Chaworths, and, if so, his connection with Walesby will account for his allegiance to the Honour of de Busli, and for his tenure of Marnham under that family, at the same time drawing closer the bonds between the family of Caus and Chaworth, a tie which is difficult to explain, and which has not, indeed, been hitherto indicated.

This land was probably that for which the mother of William de Curci fined in 11 Henry II. Unfortunately no details of that transaction are given in the Pipe Roll. The fridbor (frank-pledge) of Robert de Chauces answered for him in 21 Henry II. (see Pipe Roll), and the name of William de Chaucis appears in another Roll of 28 Henry II. This certificate may have been given at any time between those two dates : it has hardly the precise character of the returns made earlier in the reign of this king.

CHAPTER XI.

No. 8.—In the Honour of William Peverel there are sixty knights' fees and a half.

(The particulars of the Honour will be found in the Testa de Nevil.)

CHAPTER XII

Ro. 9—The Certificate of William Briwere.

WILLIAM BRIWERE, HALF A KNIGHT'S FEE FOR
CHESTERFIELD AND OTHER HIS FARMS.

The great importance of this return is its date, for it is
perfectly clear from the Pipe Rolls that William Briwere had
no farm including Chesterfield prior to the reign of Richard I.
In 6 John (page 166), it appears that William Briwere then
accounted for forty marcs for having Chesterfield, according to
the tenour of the king's charter, which he holds concerning
them. In 7 John (page 167), William Briwere accounted for
£79 for the farm of Chesterfield, and owed £18 for the rent
of Witington; but, it is added, this ought not to be exacted,
because it was comprised in the farm of Chesterfield; and he
also accounted for several other farms dating from the eighth
year of King Richard, from which period he had apparently
omitted to pay his rent.

In 8 John (page 171), William Briwere is charged £8 for
Sneinton, and £79 for Chesterfield. Of this he paid the Lepers
of Chesterfield £6, and was excused the balance. This is how
great judges farmed the crown lands, and paid their rents.

At page 173 there is a rather unintelligible entry, which
can hardly be properly extracted from the Pipe Roll of 9 John,
but the purport is clear. The Lepers of the Hospital of St.
Leonards were receiving annually the sum of £6 in exchange
for the tolls of that town, which the king gave them when Earl

of Morton, and which they received by the hands of the farmers of the town (William Briwere, as such farmer, had paid it the previous year). Now the farmers (not the Hospital) accounted for 20 m. for having the king's charter to that effect.

In the scutage of the first year of Henry III., William Briwere is assessed for 1 fee in Chesterfield ; in the 13th Henry III. he is assessed at 3 fees for Chesterfield, the payment of which he was excused, as he was in the scutage of Elvain the 16th year.

In 17 Henry III. the men of Chesterfield paid 20 m. for having the king's confirmation of the charter of Wm. Briwere, their lord. (This was the son of the late Wm. Briwere, who had succeeded his father, who died this year.)

The first notice we have of William Briwere is in the 6th of Richard I. There is only one Roll prior to this year of this reign, that of the 1st of Richard, when Ralf Murdac was sheriff, and accounted for the sum of 29s. for the fair of Chesterfield, clear proof that William Briwere had then nothing to do with it. He was again sheriff for the first part of 6 Richard I., and possibly for the previous years, since he answered for the old farm.   29s. is again received for the fair of Chesterfield.

In the 7th Richard I., p. 138, William Briwere accounted for £8 for the increase or rent of Chesterfield for that year ; and the brethren of the Hospital received 60s. on account of £6 9s. which was assigned to them in exchange for their fair.

The scribe who always prepared the Pipe Rolls beforehand had left the usual entry for the payment of the 29s. for the fair which had appeared for many years, but this year it is left blank, so that it was now clear that William Briwere had got it out of the hands of the Lepers, and was farming it himself ; and this must have been by virtue of the charter he recites in the entry of 6 John, and probably at the assessment recorded by himself in this certificate, for it agrees with no other.   The charter of 6 John grants it as a rent of £79, and a subsequent charter (see Records of Chesterfield, published for Mr. Alderman Gee) assessed it at 3 knights' fees.

In 8 Richard I. we have a most important entry, which shows that under Archbishop Hubert's new regulations the assessment was greatly increased, for it is there recorded (page 141) that Wm. Briwere accounted for £7 17s. 3d., the remainder of the rents for Chesterfield, etc., for the past year, and for £38 of the

CPSIA information can be obtained
at www.ICGtesting.com
Printed in the USA
LVOW12s1736081016

507970LV00018B/321/P